W9-APR-450

Making Plant Places

Original Craft Projects for Making Containers,
Boxes, Baskets, Hangers & Stands

Making Plant Places

*Original Projects for Making Containers,
Boxes, Baskets, Hangers & Stands*

Susan McDiarmid

Illustrations by Edward R. Turner

Hartley & Marks
PUBLISHERS

Published by
HARTLEY & MARKS PUBLISHERS INC.
P. O. Box 147   3661 West Broadway
Point Roberts, WA   Vancouver, BC
98281   V6R 2B8

Text © 2000 by Susan McDiarmid
Step-by-Step and Portrait Illustrations
© 2000 by Susan McDiarmid
Photographs by Ken Mayer
Exploded View Illustrations by Hartley & Marks
All rights reserved.

Illustrations by Edward R. Turner

Except for brief reviews, no part of this book may be reproduced
in any form or by any means, electronic or mechanical, including
photocopying, recording, or by any information storage and retrieval system,
without the written permission of the publisher.

LIBRARY OF CONGRESS CATALOGING-IN-PUBLICATION DATA
McDiarmid, Susan, 1969–
    Making plant places : projects for indoor and outdoor plants /
Susan McDiarmid
      p. cm.
    ISBN 0-88179-172-5
    1. Handicraft. 2. Plant containers. I. Title.

TT157 .M4455 2000
745.5—dc21   99-050033

Design and composition by The Typeworks
Cover design by Diane McIntosh
Color pages design by Diane McIntosh
Set in Minion

Printed in the USA

For James Waring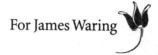

Who has shown great fortitude and courage,
even enthusiasm, at the prospect of sharing a life
filled with half-finished projects.

Contents

ACKNOWLEDGMENTS xi

INTRODUCTION xiii

PART ONE
Hanging Plants 1

    1. Ornate Wire Hanger 7
    2. Chicken Wire Hanger with Tassels 11
    3. Lacy Wire Fern Hanger 15
         Ferns 21
    4. Punched Copper and Wire Hanger 23
    5. Woven Brass and Copper Wire Hanger 27
    6. Basic Chain Hanger 31
         Trailing Vines for Indoors 33
    7. Japanese Hanging Box 35
    8. Two-Plant Mobile 39
         Perfect in Pairs 41
    9. Four-Plant Mobile 43
  10. Decoupage Wooden Ring Hanger 47
  11. Clothesline Hanger 53
  12. Beaded Cup Hanger 57
  13. Knotted Three-Pot Hanger 63
  14. Bamboo Orchid Basket 69
         Orchids 71
  15. Hanging Herb Garden Shelf 73
         Beautiful and Fragrant Herb Combinations 75
  16. Notched Pot Hanger 77
         Japanning and Other Decorative Finishes for Wood 79
  17. Weighted Water Scale Hanger 81
  18. Epiphyte Branch 85
         Some Popular Epiphytes 86
         Plant Windows 86

PART TWO

Boxes and Baskets 89

    ∾ *Seasonal Window Boxes* 93

  19. Wood Block Basket 95

  20. Wall-Mounted Plant Box 101

    ∾ *Perfect Plants for the Wall-Mounted Plant Box* 105

  21. Rustic Window Box 107

    ∾ *Liners for Baskets and Boxes* 109

  22. Edged Window Box 111

  23. Twig and Vine Planter 115

  24. Driftwood Basket 119

    ∾ *Decorative Grasses for Indoors and Outside* 121

  25. Versailles Planter 123

    ∾ *Training a Tree Standard* 126

    ∾ *Popular Plants for Topiary Standards* 126

PART THREE

Containers and Covers 127

  26. Wrapped and Woven Copper Wire Container 131

    ∾ *A Note About Succulents* 133

  27. Cloth Plant Bag 135

  28. Crown Pointed Bag 141

  29. Crocheted Plant Bag 145

    ∾ *Cacti and Succulents for a Crocheted Bag* 149

  30. Rag Bag 151

  31. Glass and Ceramic Containers 155

    ∾ *Country Charm* 157

  32. Concrete Alpine Planter (Hypertufa) 159

    ∾ *A Selection of Alpine and Miniature Plants* 165

  33. Piñata Planter 167

  34. Old Boots and Other Oddball Containers 171

    ∾ *Possible Oddball Containers* 173

  35. Painted Tin Pail Container 175

    ∾ *Painting Folk Art Flowers* 177

PART FOUR

Sconces, Stands, and Tables 181
  ∾ *Plants with Presence* 185
  36. Chicken Wire Sconce 187
  37. Chicken Wire Sconce for Two Pots 191
  38. Japanese Plant Tables 195
    ∾ *Bonsai* 199
  39. Bamboo and Raffia Plant Stand 201

PART FIVE

Frames and Trellises 205
  40. Topiary Dog 211
  41. Topiary Monkey 215
  42. Topiary Chicken 219
  43. Basic Trellis 223
  44. Redwood Trellis 227
    ∾ *Climbing Plants* 229
  45. Bamboo Teepee Trellis 231

PART SIX

Pots and More Pots 235
    ∾ *Tips on Clay Pots* 239
  46. Freehand and Traced Designs 241
  47. Crackled and Stenciled Pot 245
  48. Decoupage Pot 249
    ∾ *Sources for Images* 251
  49. Mosaic Pot 253
  50. Stacked Pot Planter 257
    ∾ *Plants for Stacked Pots* 258

PART SEVEN

Gardening Indoors with Lights 259
  51. Rolling Light Tray 265

Sources and Contributors 268

Acknowledgments

FIRST, AND MOST importantly, thank you to Scott Banta, horticulturalist and woodworker extraordinaire. Scott has been my co-pilot on this project and his contribution has been invaluable. I awaited the arrival of Scott's projects with an anticipation only slightly less keen than the one I used to feel Christmas morning, and I was never disappointed. Scott was instrumental in preparing for photo shoots and ever patient and generous with advice for his "horticulturally challenged" sister. In short, this book couldn't have happened without his help.

Thanks also to the other contributors: Aaron Banta for his woodworking talent, craft designer Gail Hourigan for her creative innovations in cloth, Syd Thomson for his ingenious hanger, Sophie Rolland for her exacting beading, Jeanne Patton for her advice, assistance, and panache with the hedge clippers, and Abby Ruoff for her generosity.

A sincere thanks to illustrator Edward R. Turner not just for his excellent illustrations and his artistic versatility, but also for his advice and expertise in all phases of the book. Ted is truly a master craftsman.

Thank you to Ken Mayer for the outstanding photography and for making the photo shoots such a lot of fun.

I am grateful to Diane McIntosh for her design of the cover and the color sections. Her talents are completely original and seemingly without limits.

Undying gratitude to John McKercher and Brent Campbell, typesetters, for contributing to the design and helping to make the book a reality.

My appreciation also to Elizabeth McLean for her excellent

copy editing skills and sense of humor, and Glenda Wilshire for her proofreading and fact-checking. Thanks to publisher Vic Marks for the very special book design and for his support of the project, and to Supriti Bharma for her enthusiasm and encouragement and contribution to the design.

I would also like to thank the staff in the many craft, hardware, and gardening stores and nurseries I have haunted for the past year. Many were very generous with their advice and help, in particular the staff at Gardenworks on Granville, Shannon Home Hardware on West Boulevard in Vancouver, Home Depot in Richmond, and Grand Prix Toys and Hobby in Vancouver. A sincere thanks to Southlands Nursery for being the most beautiful plant place in Vancouver. The staff at Southlands use their rare and beautiful plants to create an environment that never fails to inspire.

Thank you to family and friends for help of a thousand kinds—Greg and Terry McDiarmid, Carl Banta, Trevor Juby, Michelle Rae, and Kathy Waring—and finally, a sincere thanks to my mother, Wendy Banta, whose wonderful plants are a testament to her green thumb.

Introduction

THERE IS A SAYING in the publishing world that people write the books they can't find in the bookstore. That is very much the story behind this book. I love plants of all kinds but am particularly drawn to leafy wonders of the dangling persuasion—hanging plants. Some time ago I found a magnificent orchid cactus in full bloom. I bought it envisioning a showpiece in the corner of my living room. Once I had the hook screwed into the ceiling I clambered up on a chair, hung my plant, and stepped back to admire. Unfortunately, the white underside of the pot was all that could be seen. The profusions of shocking pink blossoms, cascading down the thick ropy stems, were entirely obscured from view by the angle and height of the pot. The pot was suspended a foot from the ceiling so that only the very tips of the large spiked leaves could be seen from the floor. Not only was the pot hung too high for humans to view, it was also higher than the windows, preventing the sun from reaching the plant. Plant stores frequently have fluorescent overhead lighting or skylights, so the "plant on the roof" arrangement works well. But most of us don't have our homes set up in this way, which makes hanging our plants with standard planters a problem.

So I embarked on a hunt for a suitable plant hanger. After scouring plant stores and asking all of my plant-loving friends for suggestions I came to the conclusion that I had three choices. The first, leaving the plant with its built-in hanger pot, was not an option. The second, buying an iron hanger much more expensive than the plant, did not appeal. And the third, that old Seventies favorite—the macramé hanger from a thrift store—was not to my taste. My precious plant was not going to be set off to its best advantage in a hairy orange cradle. I am not like my mother, whose green thumb is such that she could suspend her plants in garbage bins and they would still look vigorous and showy. I knew from experience that any plants under my care were unlikely to thrive in quite the same way. Of course, there was another option—I could make my own hanger. I could create a plant hanger that would fit not only my décor, but also my plant.

You can guess where I am going with this. There were so many materials and crafts from which to choose. A beaded hanger would be fabulous , as would a wire hanger. What about creating a wood or bamboo hanger? In that case, why not make projects to house not just my hanging plants, but also my outside plants and my various other indoor plants? With the help of a pair of talented woodworking brothers, one of whom has studied horticulture, and other skilled craftspeople, an unlimited number of projects for gardeners developed—including Japanese-style plant tables, baskets made of wood blocks, twig window baskets, a hanging, removable plant shelf, plant mobiles, and more. If you enjoy creating your own useful art and love plants you are sure to find a plant project here that suits. If you are a dedicated craftsperson lacking a green thumb, then use the gardening tips that come with each of the projects to cultivate one hardy and tolerant plant to show off your plant place. Either way, learn new craft techniques and plant know-how while making plant places!

Part One

Hanging Plants

Hanging Plants

Hanging houseplants is an excellent way to create leafy retreats in your home without sacrificing every inch of floor and table space. A handsome plant in an attractive hanger can lend dramatic impact to an otherwise unremarkable corner. Hanging plants in groups will impart a lush tropical ambiance. Hanging a single healthy plant with a bold architectural shape, such as one of the succulents, can accent the lines of a room. Large plants with a fluid, flowing shape can distract from or hide the weak points of a room. In addition, hanging plants bring life and movement to any situation.

In spite of their benefits, hanging plants have fallen out of favor in recent years. One of the aims of this book is to help gardeners once again come to appreciate the marvelous possibilities of hanging plants. Probably, the shortage of choices in hangers has been part of the problem. This section covers a whole range of plant hanger projects in a variety of materials to suit any décor.

In the 1970s hanging plants were everywhere and people became very creative, albeit with that uniquely Seventies flair, in their methods of hanging them. Macramé was phenomenally popular at the time and widely used to create crafts around the home. Today people are rediscovering a variety of crafts: wirework, beadwork, ropework, and faux finishes are just a few of the old crafts that people are picking up. And there has certainly been no loss of enthusiasm for indoor gardening. So why not use popular crafts to create hanging homes for your beloved houseplants?

The hanger projects that follow range from wonderfully

3

simple, as in the Basic Chain Hanger, to the very elaborate Lacy Wire Fern Hanger. Choose a hanger first and then find a plant to fit, or vice versa. Make sure that your hanger will support the weight of the plant you want to suspend, and decide in advance where you want to hang your plant in order to help you determine the length of the hanger. Some of the designs are intended to be used for small plants, but many can be adapted for larger plants. Select a hanger and plant that work with the look of your room. If your room is warm and inviting, think about adding a Santa Fe-inspired hanger and suspend it over your cactus collection to add depth to the display. If your room is very simple, all clean lines and subtle colors, add a hanger and plant that enhance the feeling of sophisticated simplicity, such as an orchid in the Japanese Hanging Box.

Many types of plants can be hung, even those most averse to handling, such as burro's tail. Most people only hang drooping, trailing plants, but if you have created a lovely hanger you won't want to completely hide it from view. Choose plants that work well with your hanger and emphasize its lines. Train the leaves up or down, as suits the needs of the plant and the look of the hanger. I have hung all sorts of plants one normally wouldn't expect to see suspended and the effect is often remarkably fresh and interesting. And the plants themselves didn't object in the least. Don't restrict yourself to the plants you see hung in garden stores. If you are concerned that a plant won't tolerate being hung, ask the staff at the garden store, but in general, the only limitations are size and shape.

Before you build the hanger, consider how you want to handle drainage. Some hanging plants come in plastic pots with a saucer attached. If you are hanging a plant in a clay pot, you can glue a light plastic saucer to the bottom with waterproof silicone sealant. Choose a plastic saucer the same color (or paint one the same color) as the pot. Glue it in a few places around the base of the pot so that the bottom is not sealed. A safer and simpler option is to place a slightly smaller plastic pot, fitted with a snug saucer, into the clay pot. That way you won't get any water dripping onto the floor. The plastic pot inside the clay pot is also a good choice because it will prevent the clay pot from becoming waterlogged and heavy.

When it comes time to actually hang your plant, make sure that you install a hook that will not damage your ceiling and will safely support the weight of the plant. I recommend the ceiling hooks with wings that prevent the screw from pulling out of the ceiling. Ask at your local hardware store if you have any questions about finding the right hook for your ceiling. Remember that you need to be able to reach the plant easily in order to water it. It must be in a location where it gets the amount of light it requires, as well as the appropriate humidity.

So go wild and make an original plant hanger using your favorite craft.

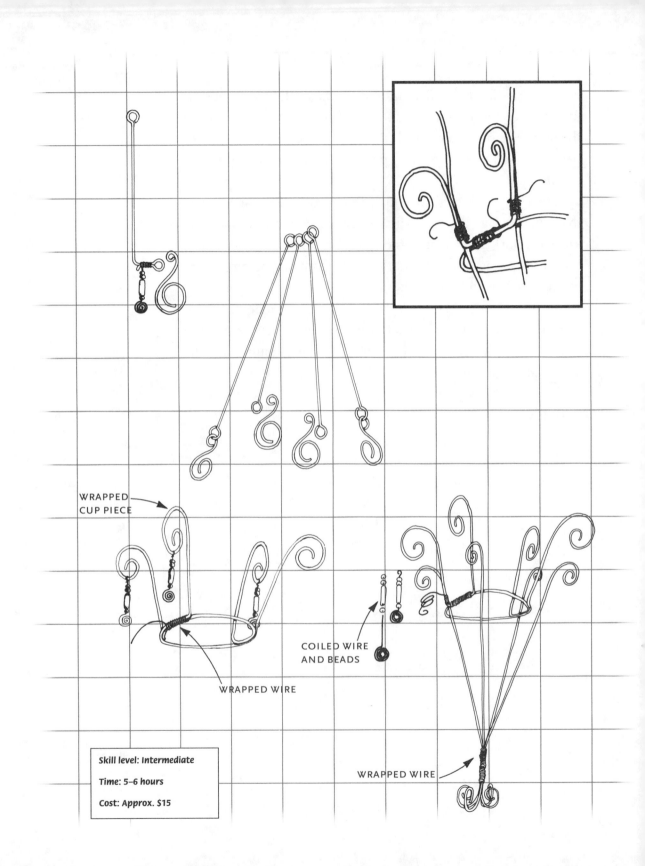

WRAPPED
CUP PIECE

WRAPPED WIRE

COILED WIRE
AND BEADS

WRAPPED WIRE

Skill level: Intermediate

Time: 5–6 hours

Cost: Approx. $15

Ornate Wire Hanger

T HIS ORNATE GOLD and silver hanger will bring a delicate elegance to any corner. Perfect for a pretty painted pot or even a short glass vase, the hanger is deceptively simple to make. Open and closed coils wrapped at the joints make the hanger sturdy as well as decorative.

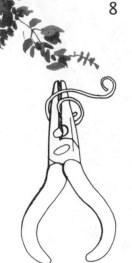

Figure 1-1

Figure 1-2

Materials

- 15-gauge galvanized wire
- 20-gauge brass wire
  Note: The wire should be available at your local hardware store.
- One 3½" diameter, 3¼" deep clay pot
- Several beads that can be threaded onto 20-gauge wire (available at beading and some craft stores)
- Clear tape

Tools

- Wire cutters
- Pliers
- Safety glasses
- Work gloves
  Note: The wire used in this project is quite heavy and you should be very careful when cutting it and working with it that you do not cut yourself.

Method

1. To begin, cut five 6" lengths of 15-gauge wire. Bend these into open coils, smaller on the top. Use your pliers to make the coils, starting at the tip of the wire and gradually working it into an even, open coil. Leave the top open slightly to hook through the bars (Figure 1-1).
2. Cut four 12" lengths of wire. Using your pliers, make them as straight as possible. Then bend a loop on the top and a loop on the bottom. These pieces will hook through the open coils (Figure 1-2).
3. Cut one 8" length of wire and make a loop in the top and a fold in the bottom with a loop at the end (Figure 1-3).
4. Cut two 12" lengths of wire and wrap them around the pot so they overlap on either side, turning up the extra length on each side (Figure 1-4). Bend these lengths into coils.

Figure 1-3

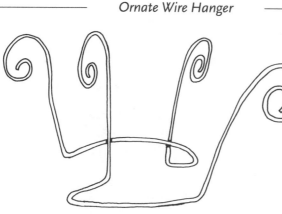

Figure 1-4

Figure 1-5

5. Take the two pieces of wire and tape them together so they cup the pot. Wrap the two sides where they are taped with brass wire to hold them securely together (Figure 1-5).

6. Cut four 15" lengths of wire. Bend the tops into wide open coils. Take the 15" lengths of wire and, one at a time, tape them to the pot supports, so that their top coils rest just below the coils of the cup piece. Wrap each of them at the taped places with brass wire.

7. Pull together the bottoms of the 15" lengths and wrap them with tape. Cover the tape with 20-gauge brass wire.

8. Make the straight ends into tight coils as shown (Figure 1-6).

9. Hook all the pieces together as shown, closing up the gaps so that the loops stay together.

10. Make five tight coils with a short length of brass wire, thread the wire with beads, and form loops at the top to attach to the larger coils.

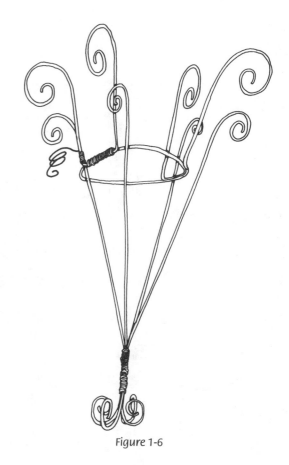

Figure 1-6

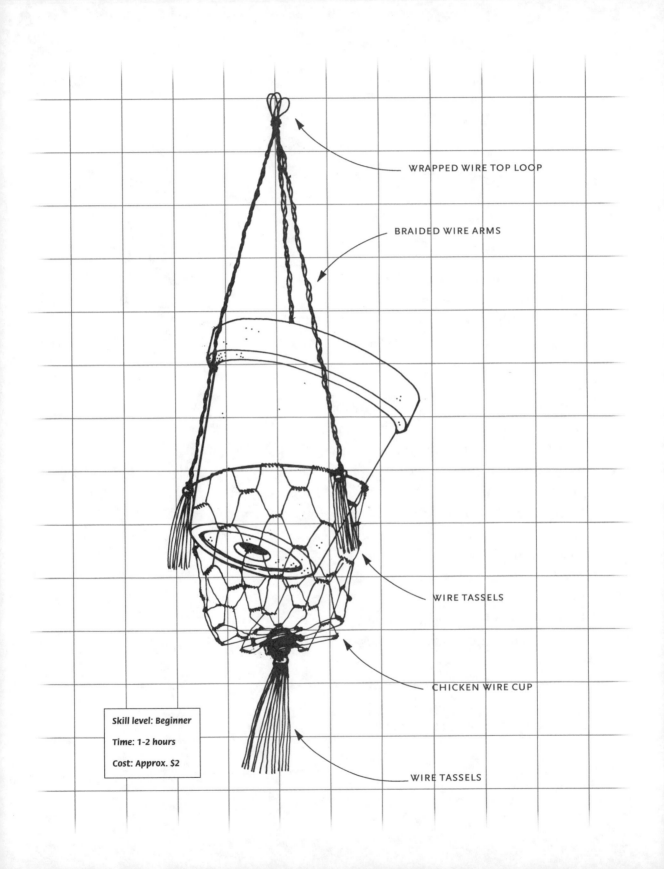

WRAPPED WIRE TOP LOOP

BRAIDED WIRE ARMS

WIRE TASSELS

CHICKEN WIRE CUP

WIRE TASSELS

Skill level: Beginner

Time: 1-2 hours

Cost: Approx. $2

Chicken Wire Hanger with Tassels

CHICKEN WIRE makes a simple and surprisingly stylish option for plant hangers. This hanger can be easily adapted to most pots and looks attractive holding a wide variety of plants. The wire tassels give it a whimsical but very modern appearance and best of all, you can make this hanger in no time!

Materials

- Approximately 1½' of chicken wire
- 20-gauge silver craft wire
- Pot

Tools

- Wire cutters
- Work gloves
- Pliers

Method

1. Wrap the length of chicken wire around the pot you want to hang, keeping the finished edge under the lip of the pot. If you like, you can place a close-fitting saucer under the pot and adjust the chicken wire to accommodate both.
2. Close up the sides of the wire by twisting the cut ends together. This will form a seam down the side of the wire cylinder.
3. Tuck and squeeze the bottom of the chicken wire so that it closes to form the base of the hanger. Secure this base in the middle with silver wire (Figure 2-1).
4. Continuing from the base of the hanger, wrap silver wire over and under the chicken wire at the bottom of the hanger, and then around and around forming a cone of wrapped wire on the very bottom (Figure 2-2).
5. Cut three 5' lengths of silver wire and braid them together (Figure 2-3).
6. Cut the braided wire into three equal parts and fasten the ends of the three parts at equal distances along the top edge of the hanger.
7. Cut at least 15 pieces of wire into 4" lengths and bend each of the pieces in half. Loop a piece of wire through the bent pieces, and secure the tassel to the wire spiral at the base of the hanger.

Figure 2-1

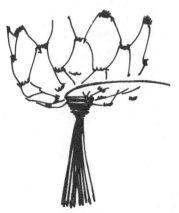

Figure 2-2

8. Cut 21 pieces of wire, each 3" long, and bend them in half. Divide the bent pieces into three groups and make three more tassels. Insert the tassels into the braided hanger arms where they meet the hanger. Make sure the arms and the tassels are very securely fastened.

Figure 2-3   Figure 2-4   Figure 2-5

Chicken Wire with a Twist

You can change the look of chicken wire by using pliers to change the shape of the holes.

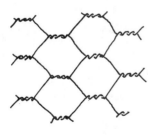

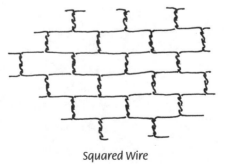

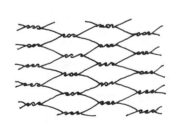

Standard Wire   Squared Wire   Squeezed Wire

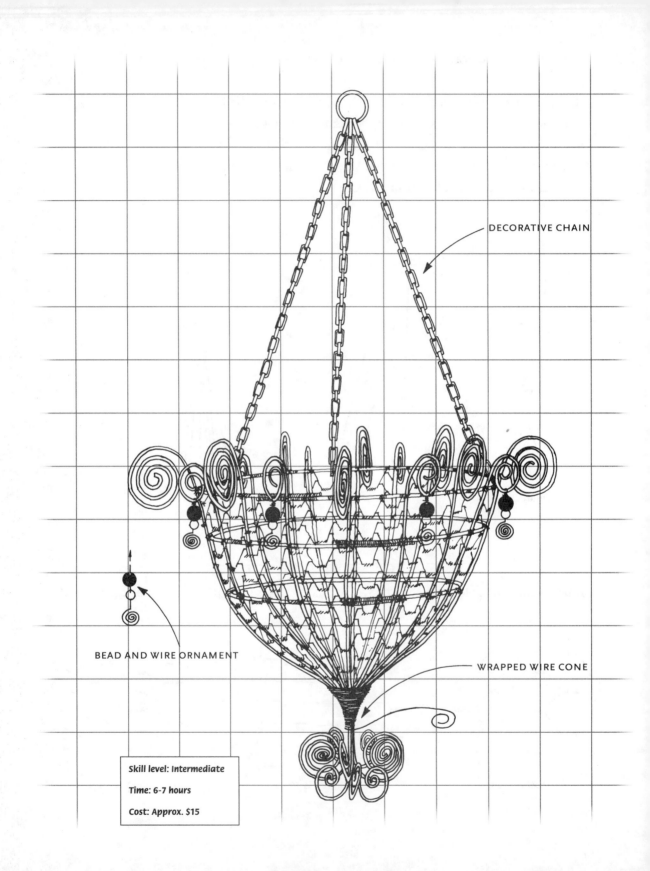

DECORATIVE CHAIN

BEAD AND WIRE ORNAMENT

WRAPPED WIRE CONE

Skill level: Intermediate

Time: 6-7 hours

Cost: Approx. $15

Lacy Wire Fern Hanger

FASHIONABLE GARDENING shops and nurseries sometimes carry Victorian-style plant hangers. These wonderfully ornate wrought iron hangers make impressive display places for ferns and other plants. They also boast impressive price tags. You can create your own fabulous fern hanger for only a few dollars using wire and beads and it will likely be just as impressive as the imported version from Europe.

Materials
- 14-gauge wire
- 16-gauge wire
- Chicken wire
- Decorative chain
- Silver craft wire (available at hardware stores and beading stores)
- A selection of beads

Tools
- Pliers
- Wire cutters
- Work gloves

Wire Wrapped Overlap

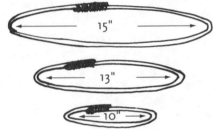

Figure 3-1

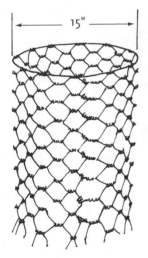

Figure 3-2

Method

1. Make three rings, one 10" in diameter, one 13" in diameter, and one 15" in diameter out of the 14-gauge wire. Form each ring leaving a long overlap. Secure the rings by wrapping them with craft wire (Figure 3-1).
2. Take the chicken wire and form it into a tube into which the 15" ring will just fit comfortably. Join the sides of the chicken wire tube by twisting the cut ends together. Trim the joined tube so it is about 1½' long (Figure 3-2).
3. Fasten the large ring to the finished edge of the chicken wire by wrapping it with silver craft wire.
4. Starting at the top, begin forming the chicken wire into "V" shapes. To do this, bend up the wire on either side of the joint so that a "V" shape is formed in the middle as the wire is squeezed together (Figure 3-3). Work your way around the chicken wire tube, row by row.

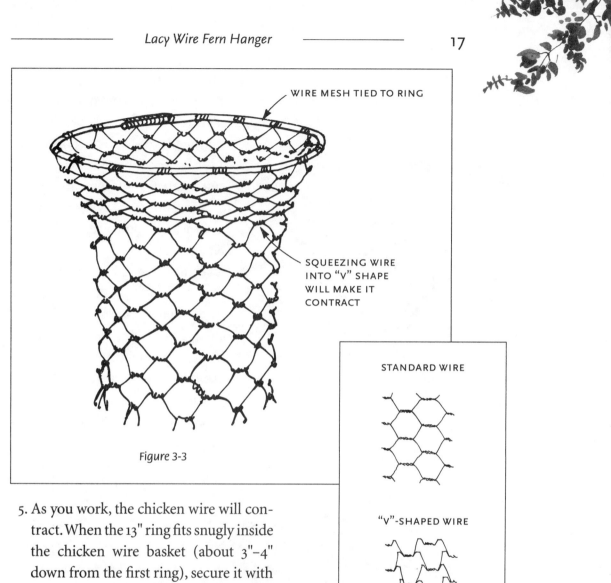

WIRE MESH TIED TO RING

SQUEEZING WIRE INTO "V" SHAPE WILL MAKE IT CONTRACT

Figure 3-3

STANDARD WIRE

"V"-SHAPED WIRE

5. As you work, the chicken wire will contract. When the 13" ring fits snugly inside the chicken wire basket (about 3"–4" down from the first ring), secure it with silver craft wire. Make sure the smaller ring is centered under the larger ring.

6. Continue working your way around the chicken wire basket, shaping it as you go. When the smallest wire ring fits comfortably into the basket (about 3"–4" down from the second ring), secure it with craft wire as you did the previous rings (Figure 3-4).

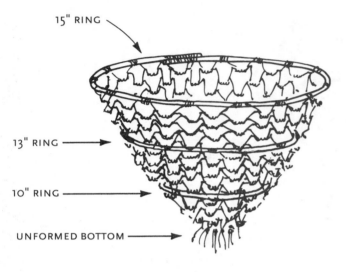

15" RING

13" RING

10" RING

UNFORMED BOTTOM

Figure 3-4

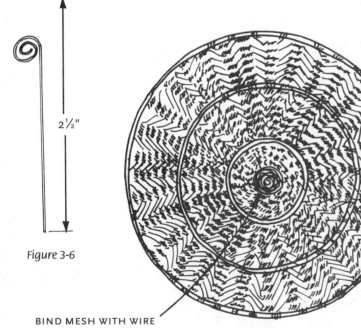

2½"

Figure 3-6

BIND MESH WITH WIRE

Figure 3-5

7. Now form the rounded bottom of the basket. Keep working the chicken wire into "V"s and use your hands to shape the bottom of the basket. When it is flat and joined, thread craft wire around the joined bottom in a circular pattern to reinforce the closure (Figure 3-5).

8. Cut eight 2½' lengths of 16-gauge wire.

9. Use your pliers to bend curls into one end of each piece. Each curl should be slightly open and wrapped around 1½ times (Figure 3-6).

10. Fasten the curled tops of the wire pieces to the top of the basket at even intervals using silver craft wire around the rim and the wire piece. The wire curls should be threaded through the rim and extend down the outside of the basket.

11. Attach the wire pieces to the second wire rim on the outside of the basket using craft wire. Make sure each of the curls is evenly aligned height at the top of the basket.

12. Now use your pliers to bend the wire pieces down so that they touch the third ring. Join them to the ring with craft wire.

13. Using your pliers, bend each of the wire pieces so that they meet at the bottom of the basket in the middle. Bend each of the straight ends into eight curls. The curls should be staggered so that they point in opposing directions and are positioned at different heights (Figure 3-7).

14. Wrap the wire pieces where they meet under the basket with craft wire until you have formed a wire cone, extending down the length of the pieces (Figure 3-8).

15. Cut eight 1½' pieces of 16-gauge wire. Bend the tops into tight curls that wrap around each other 3½ times.

16. One at a time, stick the straight ends of the wires into the top of the wrapped silver cone at the base of the basket at equals intervals, between the first eight "spokes." Use your pliers to bend the wires around the shape of the basket, fastening them at each wire ring, and keeping the ends tucked them inside the wrapped cone at the base of the basket (Figure 3-8).

17. Cut eight pieces of craft wire and coil one end tightly. Thread beads onto the straight ends of the wire and fashion the ends into loops (Figure 3-9). Fit the beaded wires over the open loops at the top of the basket.

18. Cut the decorative chain into three 3½' lengths and fasten the pieces at even distances to the rim of the basket.

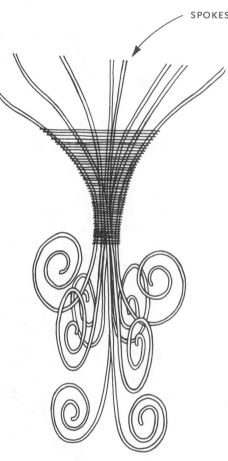

SPOKES

Figure 3-7

19. Join the three lengths of chain to the final length of chain with silver craft wire.
20. Hang the basket from a very secure hook.

This hanger is ideal for displaying ferns and other "spraying" plants. You can also hang it outside.

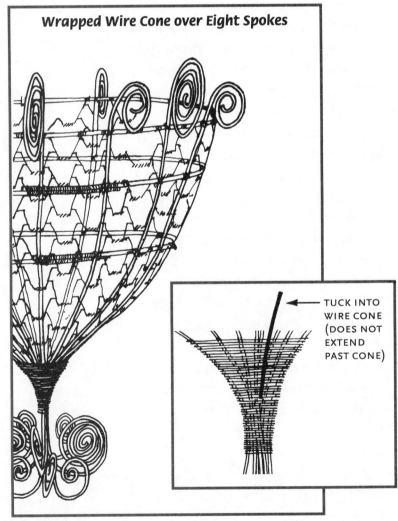

Wrapped Wire Cone over Eight Spokes

TUCK INTO WIRE CONE (DOES NOT EXTEND PAST CONE)

Figure 3-8

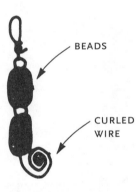

BEADS

CURLED WIRE

Figure 3-9

Ferns

Ferns have long been indoor favorites, offering a wide array of sizes, shapes, and leaves to suit any taste. They require dappled light or shade and prefer high humidity. They look attractive grouped with plants that require similar conditions, such as bromeliads and orchids.

Ferns are very popular in solariums and indoor greenhouses and impart a lush, tropical feel to their surroundings.

Asparagus fern	*Asparagus*	Wonderful wispy branching leaves with sizes of variations ranging from stems 1' to 6' long.
Boston fern, Sword fern	*Nephrolepis*	Lacy, ruffled foliage.
Christmas fern	*Polystichum*	Evergreen fern, native to North America.
Davallia	*Davallia*	Epiphyte fern, perfect for plant windows and epiphyte branches (see page 85).
Holly fern	*Cyrtomium*	Large, leaf-like, glossy green fronds, tolerant of dry air and drafts
Maidenhair fern	*Adiantum*	Many delicate leaf variants.
Mother fern	*A. bulbiferum*	Graceful arching fine fronds bearing plantlets
Polypody fern	*Polypodium*	Members of this family look very different from one another.
Spleenwort	*Asplenium*	'Bird's nest fern', green, spear-shaped fronds around fibrous nest
Staghorn fern	*Platycerium*	Another epiphyte fern with broad, forked fronds. Works very well on epiphyte branches.
Table fern, Brake fern	*Pteris*	Popular small ferns for table tops, includes variegated versions.

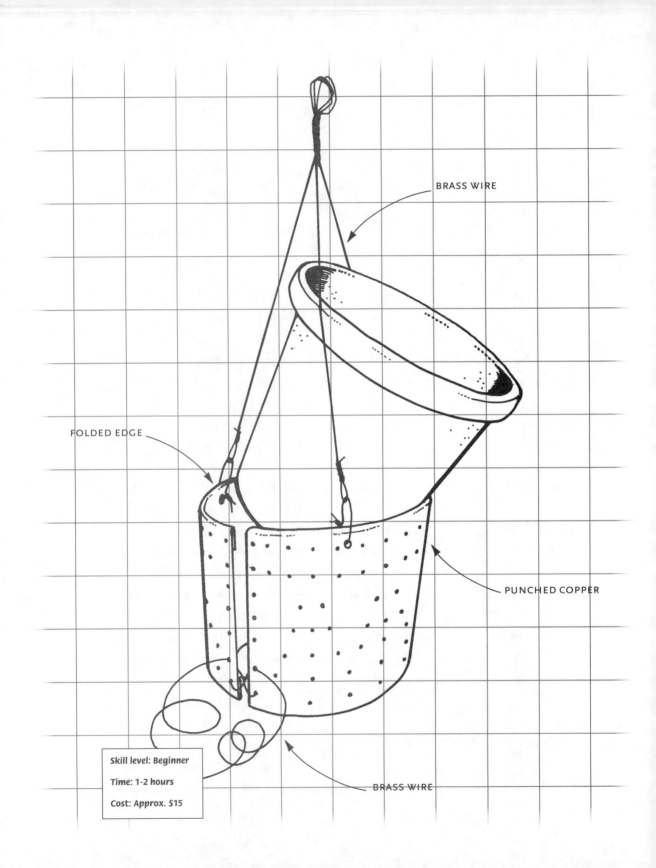

BRASS WIRE

FOLDED EDGE

PUNCHED COPPER

BRASS WIRE

Skill level: Beginner

Time: 1-2 hours

Cost: Approx. $15

Punched
Copper and
Wire Hanger

T HIS PUNCHED copper hanger has a burnished and
robust look. It is perfect for oddly shaped succulents
that are upright enough that they don't completely obscure
the patterns punched into the sheeting. Punched tin and
copper insets are traditional decorative accents on folk art
furniture and folk art objects. You can have a lot of fun re-
searching antique patterns for your piece of copper.
Choose patterns that reflect the style of your home or even
your plant. You can substitute tin sheeting for copper sheeting if you prefer.

Materials

- A pot with straight sides and a lip at the top (and no drainage hole in the bottom). This project uses a Mexican-style clay pot.
- Piece of copper sheeting 2" higher and the exact length of the diameter of the pot. (Copper sheeting is available at sheet metal supply companies and some hardware stores.)
- 18-gauge brass wire
- Paper
- Fine-point black felt pen

Tools

- Wire cutters
- Work gloves
- Safety glasses
- Pliers
- Hammer
- Standard nail
- Work surface you can nail into (such as a workbench or a large board)

Method

1. Measure your pot and cut the copper sheeting so that it is 2" higher and the same diameter as your pot. Make sure to wear work gloves and safety glasses when cutting the sheeting as it is very easy to seriously cut yourself on sheet metal.

2. Use pliers to fold the top and bottom of the copper to form a hem approximately 1" wide at top and bottom. To make the folds, use your pliers to bend the copper hems so they are at 90°. You can then use your pliers or a hammer to fold the hems flush with the copper (Figure 4-1).

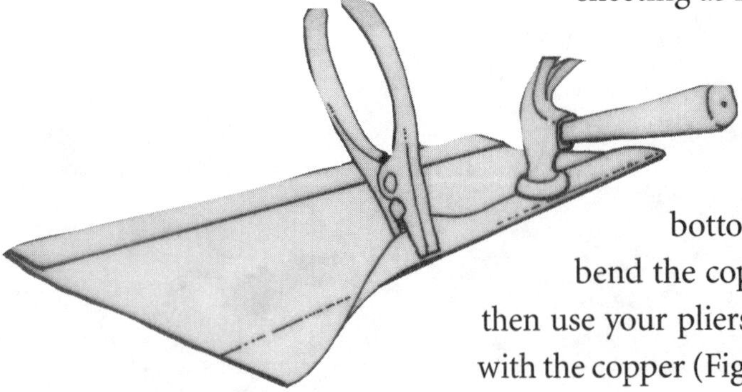

Figure 4-1

Note: The copper ring will end up sitting just under the lip of your pot and will be slightly shorter.

3. Decide on a pattern for your punched holes, and copy the pattern onto the piece of copper sheeting with a felt pen (Figures 4-2 and 4-3).

4. Place the piece of copper on a sturdy work surface such as a workbench or large piece of wood. Punch holes into the copper, using a nail, with the copper facing right side up. Do not punch the holes any closer together than ¼"(Figure 4-4).

5. When the pattern has been punched into the sheeting, punch three holes into the top of the copper, equal distances apart. Thread a length of 18-gauge brass wire through each of the holes and fasten the wires together. These will attach the hanger to the ceiling.

6. Punch holes 2" apart at each side of the sheeting, starting 1" from the bottom. Thread brass wire through the two sides, just as if you were tying a shoe, to form the copper into a circle. Tie the brass wire into a bow or knot and let the ends dangle (Figure 4-5).

7. Slip the pot into the hanger, and then place a smaller pot containing a plant inside the larger pot.

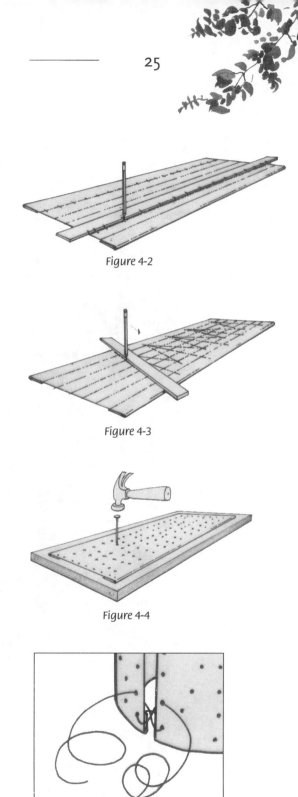

Figure 4-2

Figure 4-3

Figure 4-4

Figure 4-5

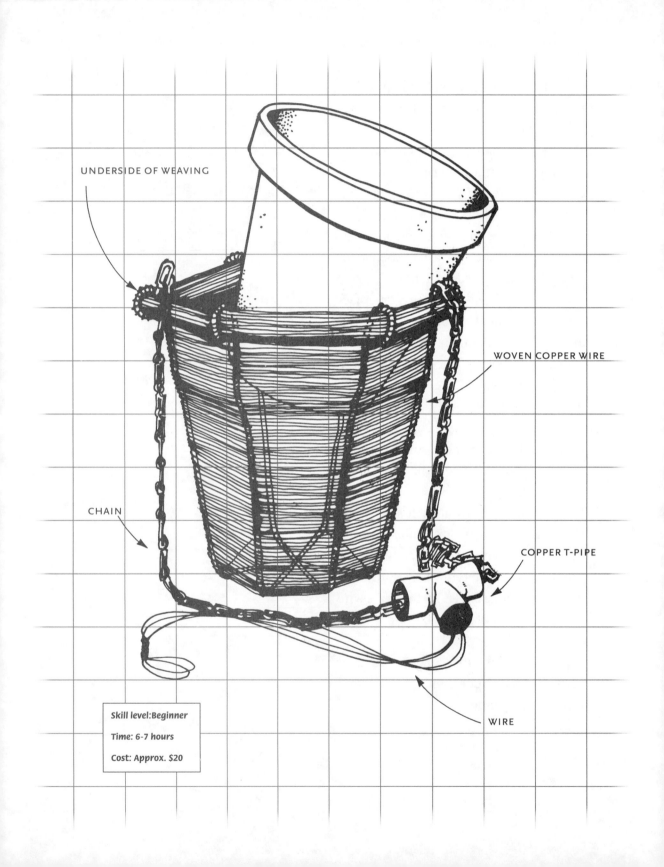

UNDERSIDE OF WEAVING

WOVEN COPPER WIRE

CHAIN

COPPER T-PIPE

WIRE

Skill level:Beginner

Time: 6-7 hours

Cost: Approx. $20

Woven Brass and Copper Wire Hanger

THIS WOVEN BRASS and copper wire hanger is the last word in funky elegance. The rich colors of the metal look wonderful against the lush green of a plant. This hanger uses chain and a piece of copper tubing to pick up the colors of the weaving and the red clay pot inside. This project is simple to make but not an afternoon's project unless you are the bionic wire weaver with fingers of steel. Give yourself a few evenings of weaving in front of the TV and you will find yourself with a marvelously ornate hanger that manages to look modern and antique at the same time.

27

Materials

- 25' of 20-gauge copper wire
- 25' of 20-gauge brass wire
- Three 14" pieces of 18-gauge galvanized wire
- One copper "T"
- 5' small-link brass chain
- One 3½" diameter, 3¼" deep clay pot
- Masking tape

  Note: The pot shown here is quite small. If you choose to weave around a larger clay pot, make sure your hook is securely fastened in the ceiling as the wire will greatly increase the weight of your potted plant. Another option is to weave around a plastic pot.

Figure 5-1

Tools

- Wire cutters
- Pliers
- Work gloves

  Note: Use gloves and glasses when cutting heavy gauge wire.

Method

1. Bend each of your three pieces of galvanized wire around your upside-down pot, one at a time, so that they cup it from the bottom. There should be wire protruding above the top of the pot (Figure 5-1). Fold down each of the top pieces so that your pot fits securely in the wire cup.
2. Fasten the wire struts at the top of the pot with masking tape to hold them securely against the pot. You may need someone to hold them in place while you tape them (Figure 5-2).
3. Taking a generous length of copper wire, wrap it around the bottom struts. Begin weaving around the struts at the bottom of the pot, working your way up (Figure 5-3).

Figure 5-2

4. Continue weaving until you reach the end of the length of wire. Wrap the end of the wire around a strut and trim it closely with your wire cutters. Wrap a new length of wire around the same strut and carry on as before.

5. Once you have woven 1" or so up the pot, change to brass wire. Weave 1" or so of brass wire up the pot. Alternate between brass and copper wire every inch.

6. When you reach the masking tape at the top of the pot, unwrap the tape and weave carefully, keeping the struts straight, up to the top of the pot.

7. Fold out the tucked-in tops of the wire struts and, using your pliers, roll the tops of the struts into curls, facing outwards.

Figure 5-3

8. Weave up the curls so that the underside of the weaving shows (see page 28).

9. Cut the brass chain into two 1' lengths. Reserve the remaining 3' of chain. When you have woven up to the highest point of the curls, slip the two lengths of chain over two struts across from one another and then continue weaving around the chains, securing the chains in the weaving.

10. Slip the two pieces of chain through the copper "T" and attach them to a piece of wire.

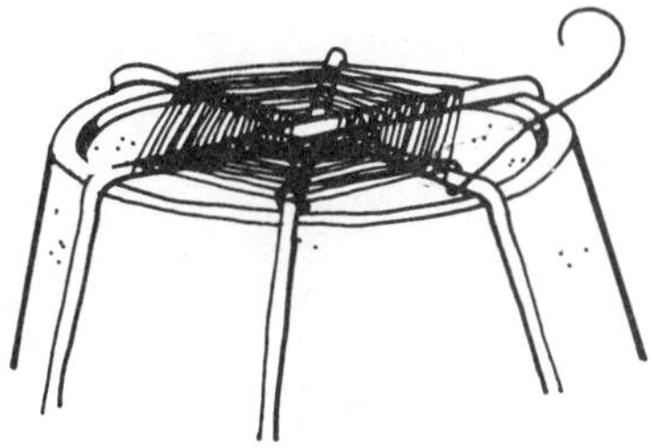

Figure 5-4

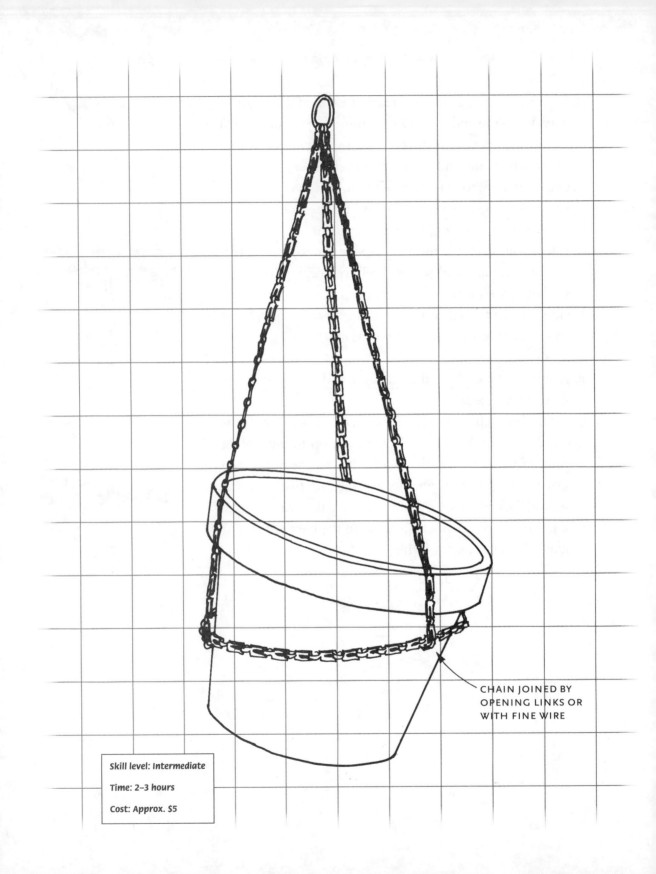

CHAIN JOINED BY
OPENING LINKS OR
WITH FINE WIRE

Skill level: Intermediate

Time: 2–3 hours

Cost: Approx. $5

Basic
Chain
Hanger

As easy and attractive
as it gets, the Basic Chain Hanger
is the perfect inexpensive solution
for hanging pots placed in lipped
containers. For this project I used a
brass container found at a yard sale
for a dollar. I brought the container
home, polished it, and fashioned a
length of brass chain into a supporting
hanger. Charmingly old-fashioned with-
out being outdated, chain hangers are unobtrusive and, depending on the type of chain you choose, will fit into any decorating
scheme.

Figure 6-1

Materials

- A container with a lip at the top that will hold your potted plant with room to spare
- A length of chain (length will depend on the size of your container and height of the ceiling). The chain should be small enough that you can cut it yourself, or you will have to measure out the lengths you need and have it cut for you at the hardware store.
- Fine wire in the same material as the chain

Figure 6-2

Tools

- Wire cutters
- Work gloves
- Pliers

Method

1. Cut a piece of chain long enough to wrap around the circumference of the pot, under the lip.
2. Join the loop of chain together with a short length of wire or by opening a link, slipping another inside it, and closing it again with pliers (Figures 6-1 and 6-2).

   Note: If you are going to use the latter method, make sure the joined links are secure and won't pull loose when you hang the plant. You may want to secure them with a small piece of wire as well.
3. Cut three lengths of chain, approximately 1' to 1½' long. Attach the three lengths at equal distances around the loop of chain (Figure 6-3).
4. Join the three lengths of chain to a single length of chain. Attach a wire loop at the top of the single length to fit over the ceiling hook.

Figure 6-3

Trailing Vines For Indoors

Bleeding heart vine	*Clerodendrum thomsoniae*
Calico flowers	*Aristolochia elegans*
Climbing onion, Zulu potato	*Bowiea volubilis*
Golden pothos	*Scindapsus aureus*
Grape ivy	*Cissus rhombifolia*
Groundsel	*Senecio herraneus, S. rowleyanus*
Heart-leaf philodendron	*Philodendron scandens*
Inch plant (Wandering Jew)	*Fluminensis variegata*
Purple bell vine	*Rhod ochiton atrosanguinium*
Rosary vine	*Ceropegia woodii*

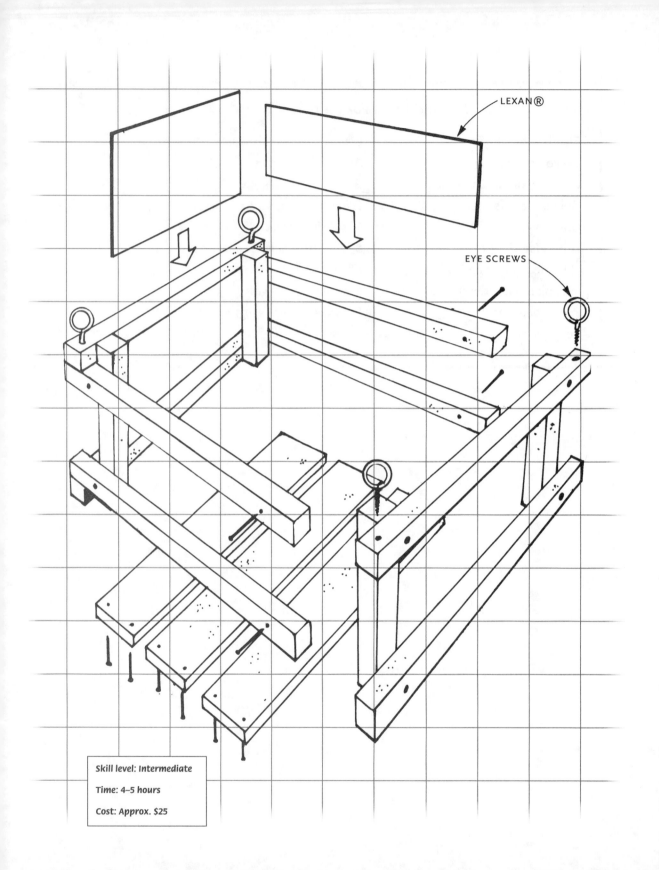

LEXAN®

EYE SCREWS

Skill level: Intermediate

Time: 4–5 hours

Cost: Approx. $25

Japanese Hanging Box

THIS ELEGANT little box is quite simple to construct and the perfect place to keep plants with an Asian flair, such as bonsai, or jade trees. The Japanese Hanging Box can be suspended from the ceiling or, placed on a table, it can serve as a decorative container. The Lexan® sides are reminiscent of Japanese paper but are waterproof and therefore more suitable for a plant container.

Design by Scott Banta

Materials

- Eight 10" × ½" × ½" pieces of wood (spruce, pine, or any other lightweight variety will be suitable)
- Four 4" × ½" × ½" pieces of wood
- Three 10" × 1½" × ¾" pieces of wood
- ⅞" nails or brads
- 4" × 31" of Lexan® (a plastic film available at plastic manufacturers. You will probably have to call around to find a dealer. Frosted plexiglas will also work.)
- Wood glue
- Eye screws (for hanging)

Tools

- Hammer
- Tablesaw (If you don't have access to a tablesaw, ask at your local lumber or hardware store. They may cut wood to size for a small fee.)

Method

1. Cut all of the pieces of wood to size.
2. Once the pieces are cut, assembly is very simple. Build two sides by nailing them together.
3. Put a spot of glue on the 4" pieces and use another ½" square piece to measure out the overhang. Nail them together, being careful to blunt the nail first to prevent splitting. Repeat on the other side (Figure 7-1).

Figure 7-1

4. Set the sides upright and apply glue to the top ends of the 10" pieces. Place two 10" pieces on the sides and carefully nail them in place (Figure 7-2). Repeat on the other side.
5. Flip the piece over and repeat. These pieces have to be carefully nailed at an angle, so a small hammer or nail punch helps.

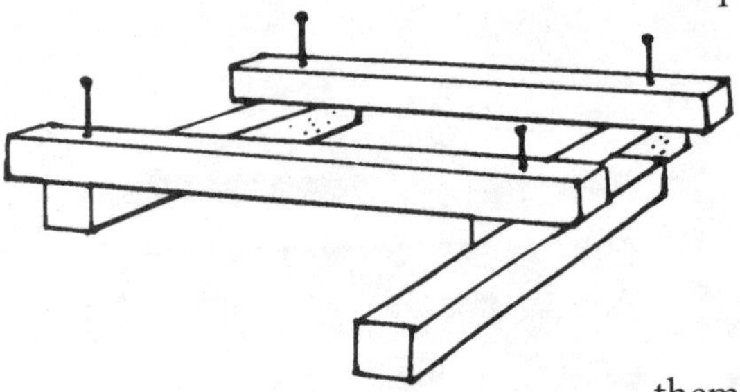

6. Glue and nail on the center bottom slat. Start by finding the center of the slat and the center of the piece to which it's being nailed. Align the marks and nail together (Figure 7-3).

7. Nail the two bottom slats 1" on either side of the center slot.

8. Paint or stain the box or leave it natural.

9. Cut two pieces of Lexan®, 7¾" × 3¾". Glue these inside the deeper sides of the box, aligned with the top and bottom slats, with the textured side facing out.

10. Cut two more pieces of Lexan®, 7¾" × 2¾". Glue these inside the other two sides of the box.

11. If you want to hang the box, screw four small eye screws on each corner.

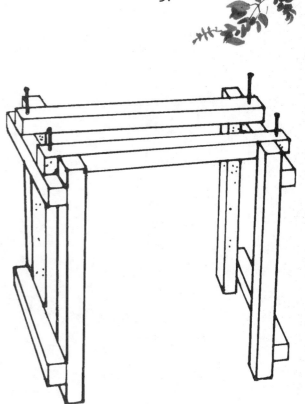

Figure 7-2

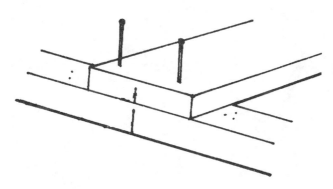

Figure 7-3

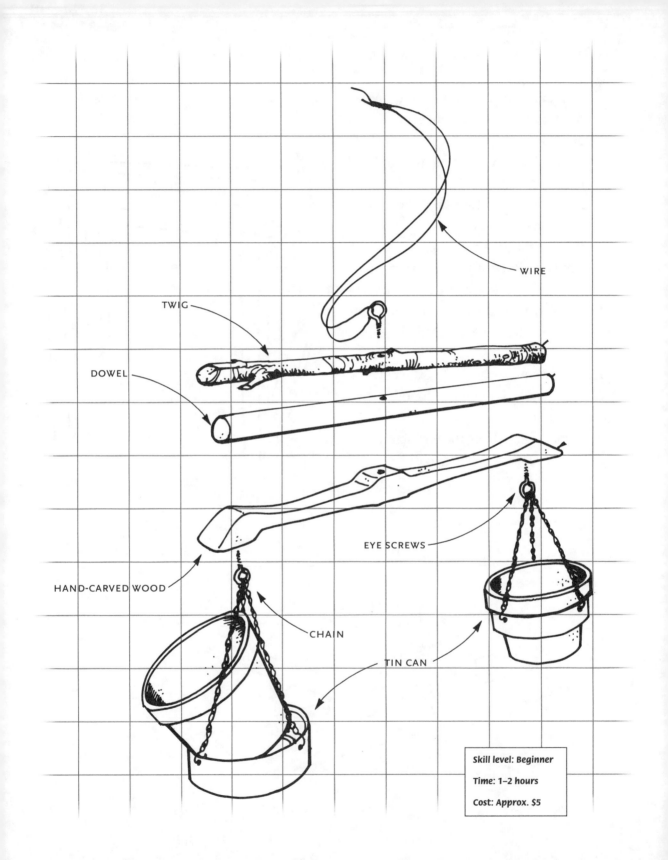

WIRE

TWIG

DOWEL

EYE SCREWS

HAND-CARVED WOOD

CHAIN

TIN CAN

Skill level: Beginner

Time: 1–2 hours

Cost: Approx. $5

Design by Scott Banta

Two-Plant Mobile

L OVELY AND SIMPLE, the wooden mobile plant hanger is
the perfect way to display a pair of matched or similar
plants. The natural and airy presentation works beautifully in
a light-filled room anywhere in the house.

Materials

- Stick, piece of doweling, or other suitable bar
- Approximately 6' of chain link, wire, or heavy string
- One large tin can (coffee cans work well)
- Three small eye screws

Tools

- Hammer
- Pliers
- Hand or electric drill, or nail
- Hacksaw
- Work gloves

Method

1. Find the center of the piece of wood and drill a hole partway through it.
2. Drill one more hole 1" from either end on the underside.
3. Screw in the eye screws to hold the chain or string on the center top and two undersides.
4. Cut the tin can in half with your hacksaw and then cut in half again (Figure 8-1).
5. Bend the sharp edges of the tin inward by rolling and turning them with your pliers. When the edges are all rolled in, they can be tapped tight against the can with a hammer if desired (Figures 8-2 and 8-3).
6. Drill or nail three holes near the top edges of each ring, equal distances from one another.
7. If you are using chain, cut it into six equal lengths and attach the chain into the holes, bending the ends of the links into hooks. If you are using string or wire, tie it through the holes. Make sure each section of chain hangs evenly.

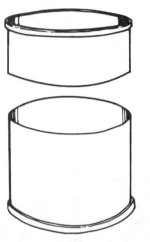

Figure 8-1

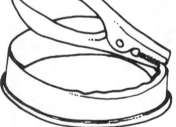

Figure 8-2

Figure 8-3

8. Attach the lengths of chain or string to two eye screws on the underside of the wood piece. Attach a single length of chain or string to the top eye screw.

9. Place pots with lips into the pot holders and hang from the ceiling.

Perfect in Pairs

Try to pair matching plants or at least similar plants. They must be the same size and weight. You can balance them out with small rocks or pebbles if necessary.

Asparagus fern	*Asparagus*
Burro's tail/Donkey's tail	*Sedum morganianum*
Christmas cactus	*Schulmbergera truncata*
English ivy	*Hedera helix*
German ivy	*Senecio mikanioides*
Golden pothos	*Epipremnum pinnatum*
Goldfish plant	*Columnea banksii*
House fern (Fishtail fern)	*Cyrtomium falcatum*
Inch plant	*Zebrina pendula*

Italian bellflower/
   Trailing campanula
    (Star of Bethlehem)
	Campanula isophylla

Lipstick vine	*Aeschynanthus radicans*
Peperomia	*Peperomia*
Heart-leaf philodendron	*Philodendron scandens*
Piggyback plant	*Tolmiea menziesii*
Spider plant	*Chlorophytum comosum*
Velvet plant	*Gynura aurantiaca sarmentosa*
Variegated wax plant	*Hoya carnosa 'variegata*

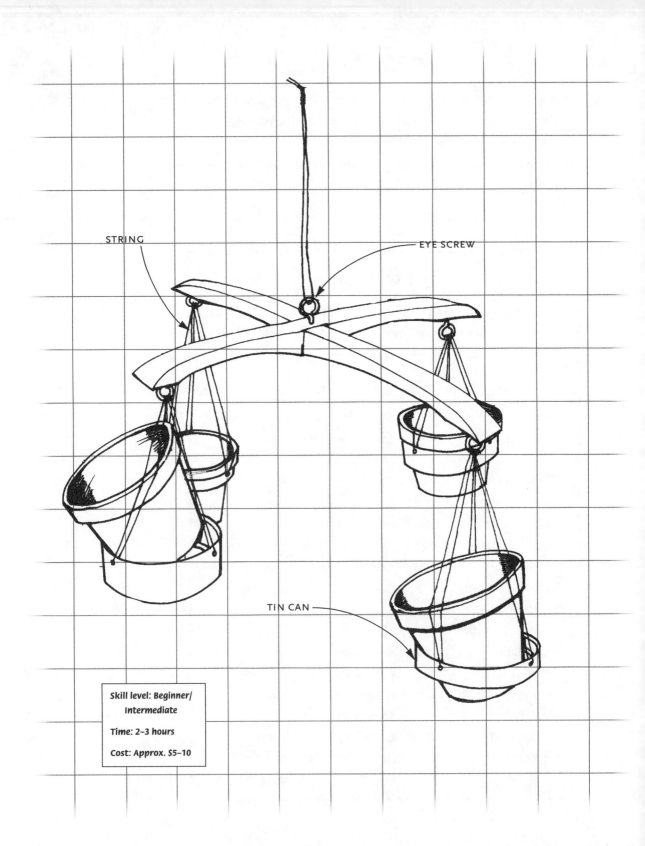

STRING

EYE SCREW

TIN CAN

Skill level: Beginner/
Intermediate

Time: 2–3 hours

Cost: Approx. $5–10

Project 9

Four-Plant Mobile

Design by Scott Banta

THIS HANGER can act like a plant chandelier or a hanging garden to charm the eye and catch the breeze. Almost as simple to construct as the Two-Plant Mobile, the four-plant version is even more impressive.

Materials

- Two sticks, pieces of doweling, or other suitable bars of the same size
- Approximately 10' of chain link, wire, or heavy string
- One large tin can (coffee cans work well)
- Five small eye screws

Tools

- Hammer
- Pliers
- Hand or electric drill, or nail
- Hacksaw
- Chisel
- Work gloves

Method

1. Find the center of the sticks and drill a hole through them. You can attach the sticks to one another by drilling through both and screwing them together, or you can make a slot on the bottom stick with a chisel so the top one fits onto it and then screw them together (Figure 9-1).
2. Drill holes 1"–2" from the ends of each stick (four more holes) on their undersides.
3. Thread in four eye screws to hold the chain or string and one on top to hang the mobile.
4. Cut the coffee can in four pieces with your hacksaw.
5. Bend the sharp edges inward by rolling and turning with your pliers. When the edges are all rolled in, they can be tapped even tighter against the can with a hammer if desired.
6. Drill or nail three holes near the top edges of each ring, equal distances from one another.
7. Attach the chain into the holes, bending the ends of the

links into hooks. Make sure each section of chain hangs evenly.

8. Attach the lengths of chain or string to the eye screws on the underside of the support pieces.

9. Place pots with lips into the pot holders and hang from the ceiling.

10. If you are worried about balancing all four pots, each of the four ends of the sticks could be attached to the ceiling with string or chain for extra support, or small rocks placed in the pots can help to even things out.

Hanger Options

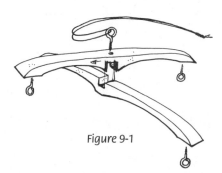

Figure 9-1

Figure 9-2

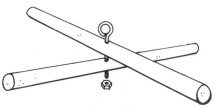

Figure 9-3

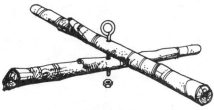

Figure 9-4

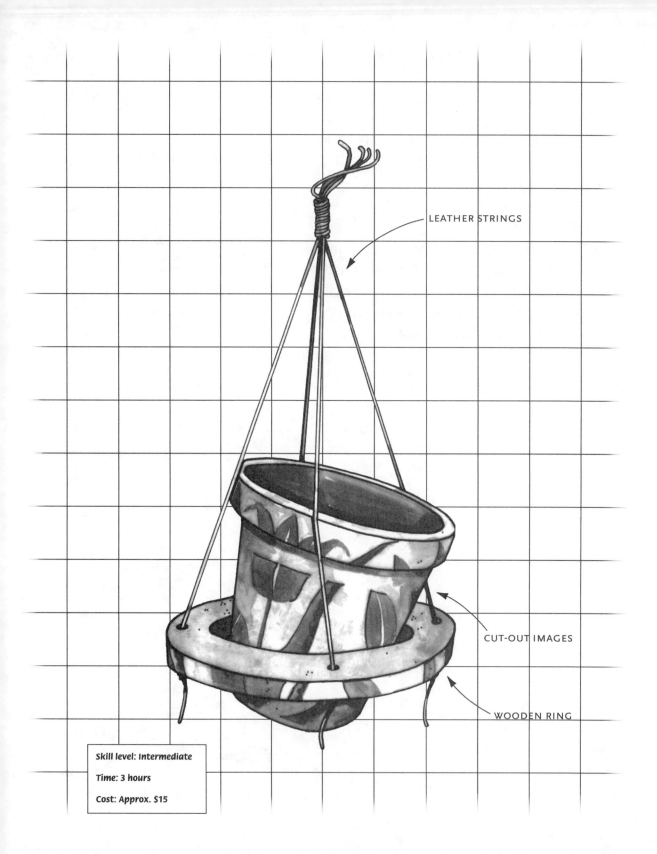

LEATHER STRINGS

CUT-OUT IMAGES

WOODEN RING

Skill level: Intermediate

Time: 3 hours

Cost: Approx. $15

Decoupage Wooden Ring Hanger

S IMPLICITY ITSELF! This simple wooden ring makes the perfect holder for a pot with a lip. Paint the ring and the pot to match, or paint a complementary design on both to show off your painting talents. Another option is to decoupage on both the pot and the ring for unique effect, as was done here. If you don't have a coping saw, try the generosity of a woodworking friend.

Design by Scott Banta

Materials

- One square piece of ¾" plywood, at least 2" wider and taller than the circumference of the pot being hung
- At least 4' of light rope, or leather string
- Three small eye screws
- Pot with a rim (preferably a clay pot)
- Images for decoupaging onto the ring and pot
- Decoupage medium
- Acrylic craft paint in desired colors
- Polyurethane varnish

Tools

- Tape measure
- Scribe
- Coping saw or scroll saw
- Drill with ½" and ⅛" bits
- File or 80 grit sandpaper
- Scissors
- Paintbrush

Method

1. With your tape measure, determine the circumference of your pot below the lip.
2. Scribe the circumference of the pot onto the piece of plywood. This will be the inside of the ring.
3. Scribe a second line ¾" outside the first circle.
4. Cut along the outside circle with the coping saw. You can sand or file imperfections later.
5. Drill a ½" hole near the inside line of the inner circle of the ring. This is the hole the coping saw will fit through. Cut carefully around this inside line.
6. Sand or file both the inside and outside surfaces of the ring. Frequently place your pot inside the ring to make sure it fits smoothly and to check your work.

Scribing a Wooden Ring

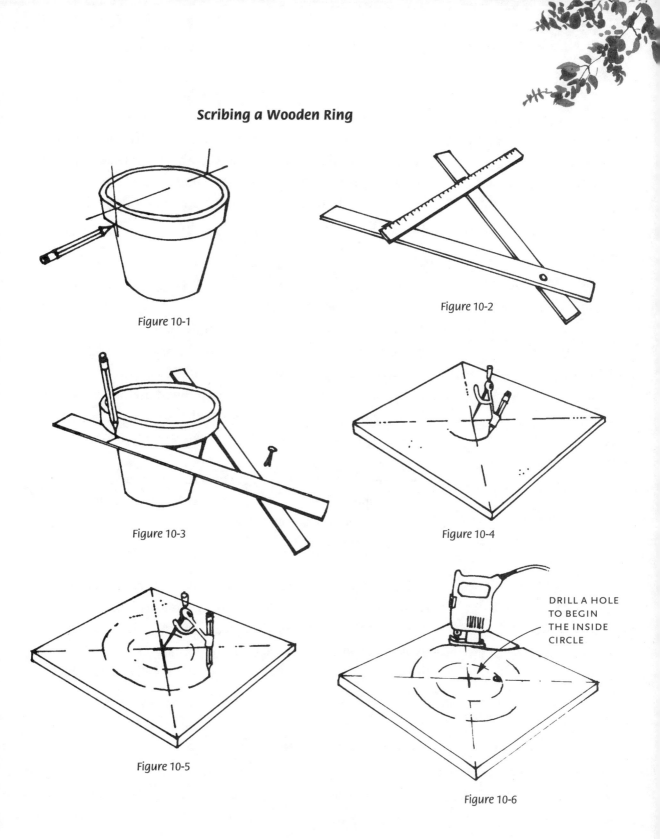

Figure 10-1

Figure 10-2

Figure 10-3

Figure 10-4

Figure 10-5

DRILL A HOLE
TO BEGIN
THE INSIDE
CIRCLE

Figure 10-6

7. Paint the entire pot and ring (separately) with a coat of acrylic paint.

8. Choose the images you want to decoupage onto your pot and ring. Arrange the images so that they appear to run from the top of the pot to the top and underside of the ring and onto the bottom of the pot in a continuous line. Cut them where the ring meets the pot so the ring is kept separate from the pot.

9. Glue your images onto the ring and pot as marked. Keep the pot and ring separate from one another as you do this so they don't get stuck together.

10. Paint over the images on the pot and the ring with decoupage medium. Allow the first coat to dry and add another coat. Keep adding coats, allowing each one to dry completely before the next is applied. Build up the finish until the varnished surface is flush with the images.

11. Paint the whole pot and ring (separately) with a coat of polyurethane varnish.

12. Drill three holes into the ring, equal distances apart, and thread approximately 1' of rope or leather through each hole, knotted at the end, and attach at the top with the remaining length of hanging material.

This simple ring hanger can become a *tour de force* of creativity with a little effort. Rather than decoupage images onto your pot and ring, you can trot out your decorative painting talents or demonstrate your eye for bold color. Choose plants that look well with your decorative finish or choose a decorative finish that complements your plant.

Decoupage

In the 18th and 19th centuries, when decoupage was a popular pastime for the upper classes, it was possible to buy books of images for japanning and decoupage. These black and white images were first colored, then cut out and pasted onto surfaces for decoupage projects or transferred onto japanned surfaces. Try enlarging and then coloring these designs and using them for a decoupage project. Old books in the library and antique book stores are also good sources for images.

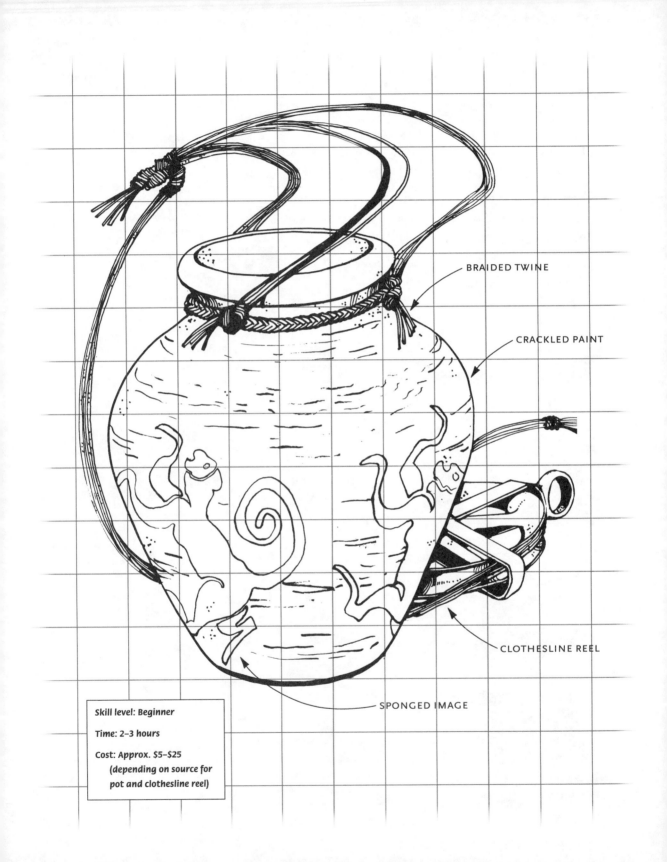

BRAIDED TWINE

CRACKLED PAINT

CLOTHESLINE REEL

SPONGED IMAGE

Skill level: Beginner

Time: 2–3 hours

Cost: Approx. $5–$25
(depending on source for
pot and clothesline reel)

Clothesline Hanger

T HE KEY to the clothesline hanger is rust! If you can't find one that has been naturally aged so that it is fashionably rusted, paint a metal clothesline reel brown and add paint to accentuate the impression of rusted metal. For complete instructions on how to paint "rust," Abby Ruoff's book *Rustic Originals* is an excellent guide. Old metal clothesline reels are often available in yard sales and flea markets, as well as in thrift stores. This project includes a crackled and sponged pot and traditional braidwork in rough twine to complete the impression of antique charm.

Materials

- Metal clothesline reel (naturally rusted or painted to appear rusted)
- Clay pot with a lip
- Natural twine or string
- Acrylic paints
- Crackling medium (available at craft and hobby stores)
- Thin sponge
- Several sheets of scrap paper
- Polyurethane spray

Tools

- Scissors
- At least two paintbrushes

Method

1. To prepare the pot, paint it with a light-colored base coat of acrylic paint. Let the paint dry.
2. Paint the light base coat with a thick coating of crackling medium. Let dry at least four hours.
   Note: The instructions on crackling medium often say to apply the third coat two to three hours after the crackling medium, but I have had much better success after four hours or longer.
3. Paint a coat of dark paint over the crackling medium. This should be applied evenly and you should not paint over any area with more than one stroke. The paint should crackle immediately, showing through to the light base coat beneath. This pot was painted dark brown with a bit of gold barely stirred in to reflect the color of the rusted clothesline reel. Let the pot dry at least overnight.

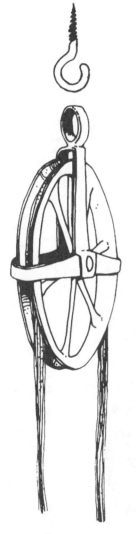

Figure 11-1

4. Cut the sponge into a desired shape. This one was cut into a monkey pattern (Figure 11-2). Dip the sponge into paint in a color that will stand out on the pot, or paint the sponge directly.

5. Press the sponge onto scrap paper several times as a test. When you are happy with the pattern the sponge leaves, press it onto the pot. Add more paint as necessary to achieve the desired opacity of print. Let the prints dry.

6. Spray the whole pot, inside and out, with a coating of polyurethane and let it dry.

7. Braid the twine and tie the braided length around the top of the pot, under the lip.

8. Cut nine lengths of twine, each 2' long, and tie them in groups of three around the braid under the lip of the pot.

9. Cut three lengths of twine at least 6' long and tie them to the tops of the three groups of twine. Thread this long length through the clothesline reel.

10. Hang the reel from a secure hook in the ceiling or other fastening and tie the end of the twine onto a nearby hook or object (Figure 11-1).

   Note: The Clothesline Hanger looks best holding flowering potted plants. It can be used indoors or outside. Set the plants, in their plastic pots, inside the painted pot.

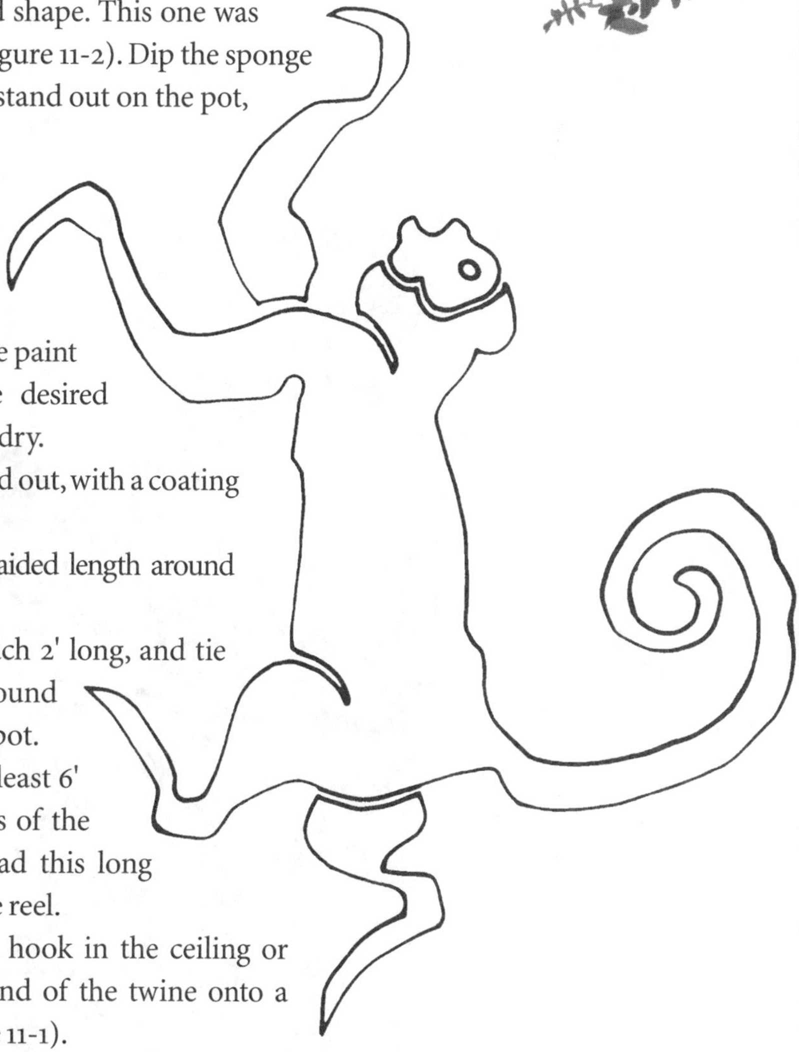

Figure 11-2

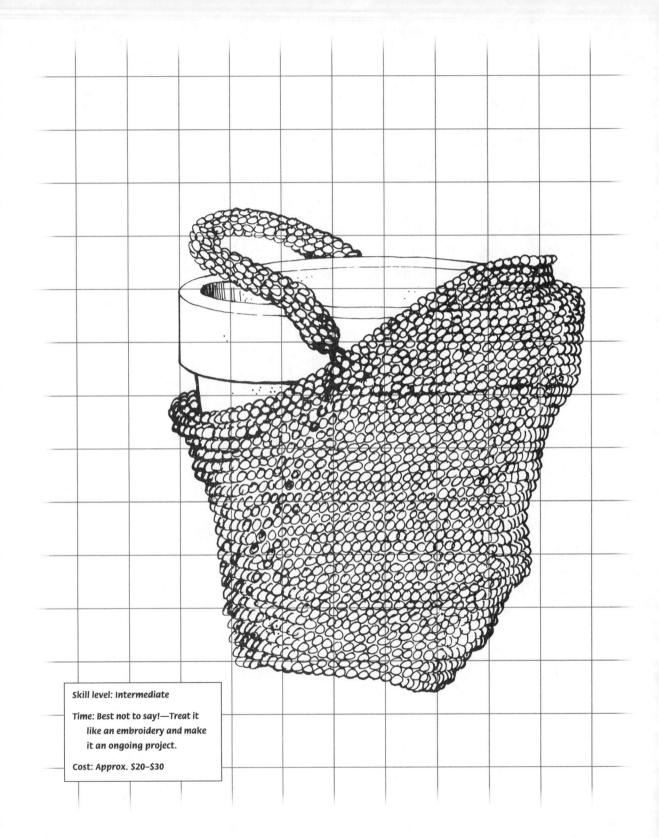

Skill level: *Intermediate*

Time: *Best not to say!—Treat it like an embroidery and make it an ongoing project.*

Cost: *Approx. $20–$30*

Beaded Cup Hanger

B EADING IS an antique craft that appeals for its intricate beauty. A beaded cup hanger will be not only a fascinating showcase for a small plant, but also a piece of art that may be valued for generations. A labor of love, the somewhat time-consuming process of bead-weaving is well worth the effort when you see the fine beaded "fabric" you can create to hold your pot. Treat the project like you would a piece of embroidery and spread the work over time.

Design by Sophie Rolland

Materials

- #10 beads (enough to cover a small pot, at least six containers)
- The strongest beading line you can find that fits comfortably through your beads and needle
- Small pot
- Tape

Tools

- Flexible beading needle that will fit through #10 beads, with the smallest eye possible (from a craft needle set versus a sewing needle set)
- Scissors

Figure 12-1

Method

1. Thread enough beads to reach around the top of the pot comfortably, leaving about ½" of bare string so that the beads are a little loose. You should have an even number of beads (Figure 12-1).
2. Tie the string closed with two square knots and tape the short end of the beading string to the top lip of the pot to keep the beads in place (Figure 12-2).
3. The original string of beads will become rows one and two once the third row is started.

Figure 12-2

4. To make the first three rows, pass your needle through the first bead to the left of the knot, add a bead, skip the next bead on the ring, and thread the next bead, continuing until you get to the end of the row. As you are working, pull the thread tight so that the beads go into their up-and-down position (Figure 12-3).

5. When you get to the end of this and every row, your needle should catch the first bead of the previous row and the first bead of the current row. (This first bead of each new row will move one space to the left.)

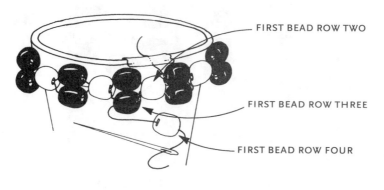

FIRST BEAD ROW TWO

FIRST BEAD ROW THREE

FIRST BEAD ROW FOUR

Figure 12-3

6. Continue down the lip of the pot in this manner.

7. When you reach the body of the pot, you will need to start decreasing. Always decrease both on the outside edges at the end of the row and in the middle of the row (you will always have an even number of beads at the end of each row).

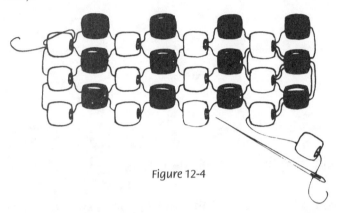

Figure 12-4

8. Depending on the shape of the pot, you will have to decrease every three or four rows. Make sure that your beading loosely follows the shape of the pot.

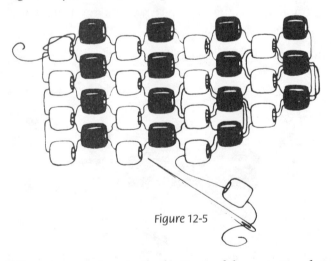

Figure 12-5

9. When you get close to the bottom of the pot, stop decreasing when you reach a number of beads that is divisible by four.

10. To make the base, divide the number of beads into four sections. Weave as usual but drop the last bead of each section. For each row you should decrease by four beads. When you get to the last four, pull the string taut and knot the string.

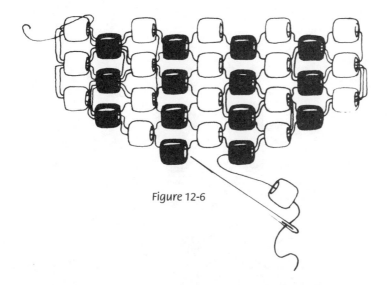

Figure 12-6

Example: If you are left with 40 beads when you are ready to make the base, divide it into 4 sections of 10 beads. Weave as usual through 9 beads and drop the 10th. At the end of the row you will have 36 beads, so you will weave 8 beads and drop the 9th. Continue in this fashion, always dropping 4 beads from each row until you have only 4 beads left, then tie off.

If done correctly, you will end up with a flat base with four straight lines converging on the center.

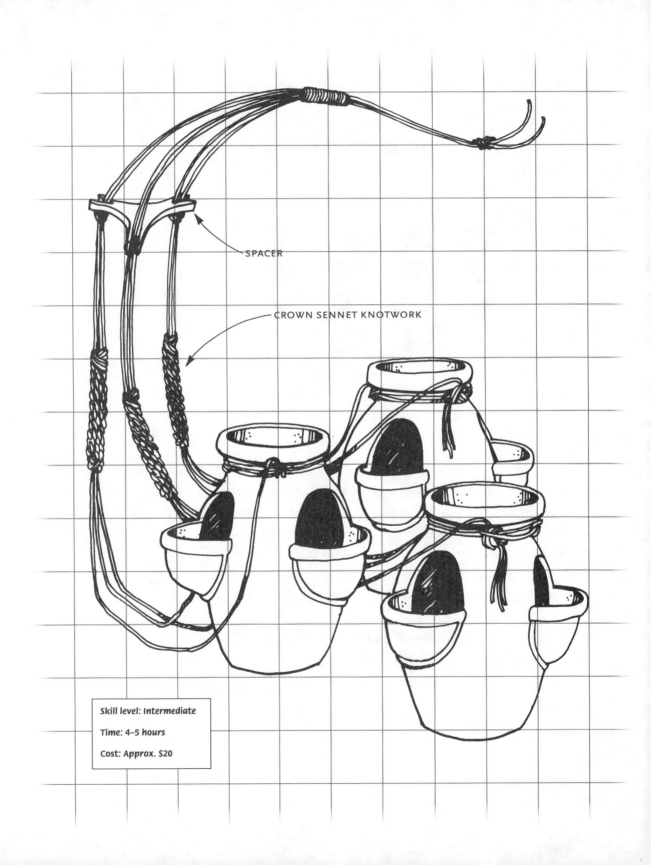

SPACER

CROWN SENNET KNOTWORK

Skill level: Intermediate

Time: 4–5 hours

Cost: Approx. $20

Knotted Three-Pot Hanger

T HIS COLLECTION of three
small pots hung with traditional knot-work is perfect for a
country kitchen or a sunny porch. You
can paint the pots with a Santa Fe pattern and dye the ropes for colorful
effect. Plant the pots with herbs or a collection of tiny cacti.

Materials

- Lightweight cotton rope
- Three clay pots with pockets and a lip at the top
- Masking tape
- Natural-colored thread
- Highlighter pens in three colors
- Acrylic paints in bold colors (optional)

Tools

- Scissors
- Fine paintbrushes

Method

1. Cut the rope into three 4' lengths and wrap one end of each of the three pieces with masking tape. Add a different highlighter color to each end to help distinguish them.
2. Using a plain overhand knot, tie the three pieces around the top of one pot, leaving the frayed ends of the ropes loose (Figure 13-1).
3. The three long ropes at the knot will be used to suspend the pot. Separate ropes B and C from either side of A and tie them equidistant from each other with two half-hitches (Figure 13-2) as shown in Figure 13-3.
4. Tie the three ropes into one knot approximately 8" up from the top of the pot.

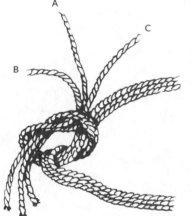

Figure 13-1

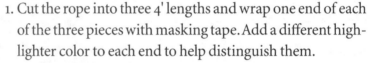

Figure 13-2

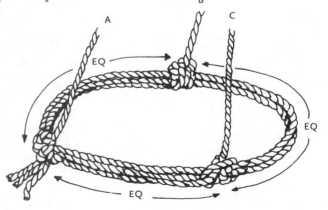

Figure 13-3

5. Begin the crown sennet knot by holding the overhand knot in your hand. Pass the first strand over the second, the second over the third, and the third back through the loop made by the first strand (Figures 13-4 to 13-7).

6. Pull the knot tight, one strand at a time so that the "crown" is even and taut (Figure 13-8).

7. Starting again with the first strand, make another crown and continue clockwise up the ropes in this manner until you have made a 5" long sennet (Figure 13-9).

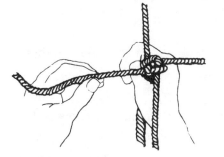

Figure 13-4

Figure 13-5

Figure 13-6

Figure 13-7

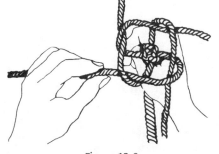

Figure 13-8

Figure 13-9

8. Repeat these steps with the two remaining pots.

9. Adjust the pots so that they sit at staggered levels and are angled slightly outwards, and tie a plain knot at the top with their extra rope (Figure 13-10).

10. Whip the ends of the ropes by taking one of the longest lengths of cord and running it back and forth, and then wrapping it as shown (Figures 13-11 and 13-12). Tuck the ends back under.

11. Cut the spacer from a piece of ¼" plywood or heavy cardboard, using the pattern provided (Figure 13-13).

12. Tie two of the rope ends to make a loop and cut the other five quite close to the whipping.

    Note: If you want to paint the pots before you tie them together, Mexican and Spanish designs and other Southwestern-style patterns look great (see Figure 13-14 for a traditional pattern). If you want to dye the ropes before you knot them, make sure to

Figure 13-10

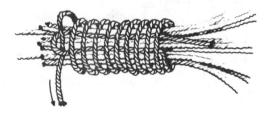

Figure 13-11

Figure 13-12

use cotton ropes, because synthetic ropes will not absorb dye. You can dye the ropes in three batches to make three different colors. These ropes can then be tied without being coded with a highlighter—you will always be able to tell one, two, and three apart!

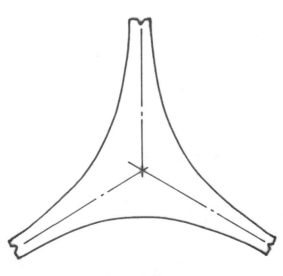

Spacer Pattern
Figure 13-13
(Suggested actual size: 8")

Traditional Design
Figure 13-14

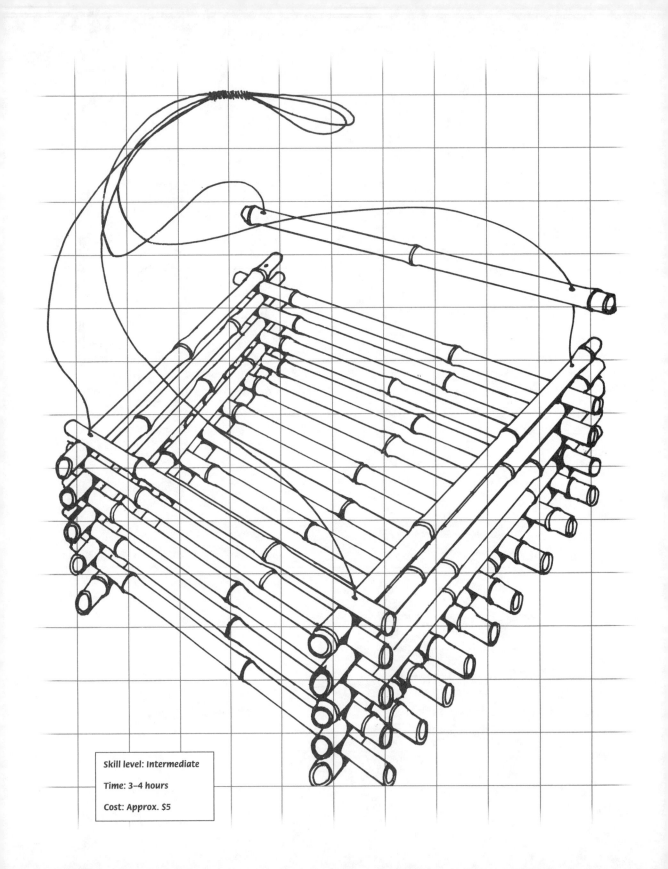

Skill level: Intermediate

Time: 3–4 hours

Cost: Approx. $5

Bamboo
Orchid
Basket

Bamboo baskets are a traditional way to display orchids, bromeliads, and other exotic tropical plants. Lined with coconut or fiber matting, bamboo baskets are perfect for housing that most rarified of indoor plants—the orchid. You will find the construction simple and the box itself inexpensive to make.

Materials

- 20-gauge galvanized wire
- Twenty-six pieces of bamboo, each 10" long

Preparing Bamboo for Drilling

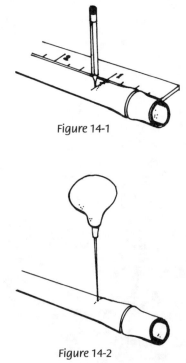

Figure 14-1

Tools

- Electric drill with a very fine bit
- Handsaw
- Scratch awl or nail

Method

1. Cut several stalks of bamboo into 10" lengths until you have 26 pieces. If you would like to build a solid rather than spaced bottom, you will need to cut at least 38 pieces.

2. Take two of the pieces of bamboo, and drill two holes 1" from the end on either end. Roll the drilled pieces over and drill another hole at right angles to the the first holes. The holes should intersect so that wires can be crossed inside the bamboo (Figure 14-4). To begin drilling holes in the slippery bamboo, make a scratch mark at the place you want to drill with either a scratch awl or a nail. The roughened area will give the drill bit a chance to grip the surface of the bamboo.

3. Now drill one hole 1" from each end in the remainder of the pieces.

4. To make the bottom of the basket, thread enough pieces onto two 4' lengths of wire to form a square bottom. (You can make a solid or spaced bottom, depending on your preference.) Place your double-drilled pieces at each end of the bottom.

5. When the bottom pieces are threaded, place two bottom supports under them and run the wire down and back into the end pieces on the bottom.

Figure 14-2

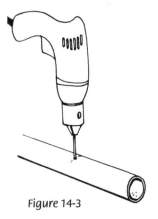

Figure 14-3

6. Run the wire back up through the double-drilled end pieces of the bottom and then begin layering on the sides of the bamboo basket.

7. When the basket is high enough, tie knots in the ends of the wire protruding from the four corners.

8. Tie the four lengths of wire together approximately 2' above the basket.

9. Line the basket with coconut matting or leave it bare and simply place a pot inside.

10. Bamboo Orchid Baskets are ideal hung in plant windows. You can also hang them from an epiphyte branch (see page 85).

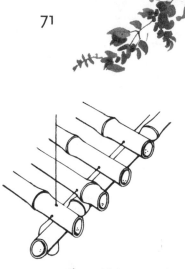

Figure 14-4

Orchids

The word orchid is synonymous with exotic beauty. The obvious attraction of the orchid is its exquisitely dramatic flower. The family Orchidicae is the largest plant family and forms the basis of many a serious gardener's obsession.

Orchids are either terrestrial (grown in the earth) or epiphytic (grown on trees). They come from the tropics or subtropics and many species are only suitable for cultivation in a greenhouse due to their very high humidity requirements. Even the orchid varieties suitable for indoor gardeners are often more challenging than most indoor plants, except perhaps bonsai.

Terrestrial orchids do best in open or latticework baskets, such as the bamboo basket, because they require very good drainage and air circulation around their roots to stay healthy. They have very particular soil requirements: standard potting soils won't work. Fern roots, sphagnum moss, fir bark, redwood bark or coconut fiber, and some commercial orchid soils are combined with gravel, clay, or rock wool to meet the needs of demanding orchids. They require frequent fertilization during their growing season and prefer a drenching/drying pattern of watering.

Orchids are an ideal choice for a plant window. For more information on plant windows see pages 86 and 87. If you receive an orchid as a gift or buy a potted orchid in bloom, make sure to find out its name so you can learn about its particular care.

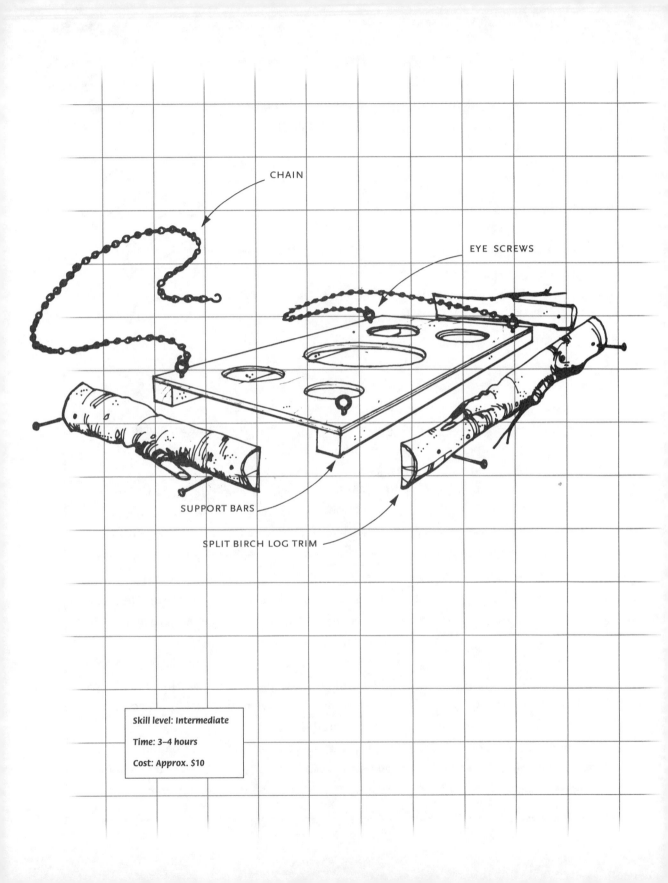

CHAIN

EYE SCREWS

SUPPORT BARS

SPLIT BIRCH LOG TRIM

Skill level: Intermediate

Time: 3–4 hours

Cost: Approx. $10

Design by Scott Banta

Hanging Herb Garden Shelf

THIS IS a wonderful way to cultivate your own herb garden, either inside or outdoors. Hung in the corner of a kitchen or some other out-of-the-way place, under a plant light, or near a window, it will save space and simplify your indoor gardening.

73

Materials

- One piece of 2' × 3½' × ¾" plywood
- Two pieces of 1" × 1" wood, each 3½' long (the length of the tray)
- Two pieces of 3' long chain
- Four 1½" #6 eye screws
- Latex paint and primer
- Polyurethane spray
- Twig trim or split birch log (optional)

Tools

- Jigsaw
- Drill with ½" and 1/8" bits
- Screwdriver
- Two paintbrushes

Method

1. Plan your shelf on a piece of paper first, according to how much space you have and the sizes of pots you want it to hold. For this project the tray holds five pots (four 6" pots and one 12" pot). Keep in mind that the pots will need some space between them to accommodate the plants and to ensure the tray doesn't get too heavy.

2. Get your piece of plywood and place your pots on it as you planned on the paper. Trace holes the right circumference to hold each pot.

3. Drill a ½" hole in the middle of each traced circle. Carefully cut out each hole. (You can ask a woodworker with a jigsaw or your local lumberyard to cut your plywood for you if you can't do it at home.) Sand or file the holes to ensure the pots fit smoothly.

4. Nail the 1" × 1" bars onto the bottom of the tray. Your tray may not need the additional support, but they will provide peace of mind.

5. Drill two holes in the front and two in the back of the shelf and attach the eye screws.

6. Paint the tray with white latex primer. Let it dry.

7. Paint the tray with latex paint in the desired color and let it dry.

8. *Optional:* You can nail a split piece of birch to the front and sides of the tray to finish it, or add twigs and vine to the edges. Needless to say, the finishing on your herb tray is a matter of taste. You can paint it a solid color or leave it plain. If your tray has a relatively flat surface, you can stencil on it or decoupage images onto it. You can also handprint the names of the herbs around the edges of their "holes." You might also want to consider painting the pots to match your hanging herb table for maximum effect. If you cannot hang your herb shelf right near a window, clip a lamp and a 60-watt grow light above it or place it by a long fluorescent plant light to keep your herbs healthy and growing.

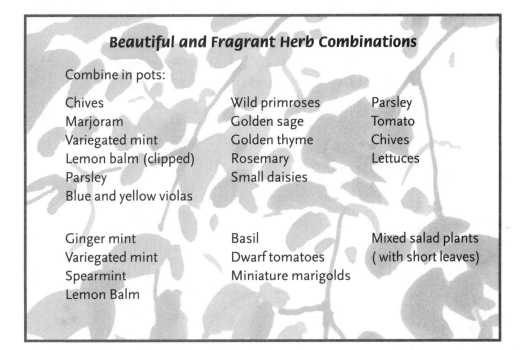

Beautiful and Fragrant Herb Combinations

Combine in pots:

Chives	Wild primroses	Parsley
Marjoram	Golden sage	Tomato
Variegated mint	Golden thyme	Chives
Lemon balm (clipped)	Rosemary	Lettuces
Parsley	Small daisies	
Blue and yellow violas		
Ginger mint	Basil	Mixed salad plants
Variegated mint	Dwarf tomatoes	(with short leaves)
Spearmint	Miniature marigolds	
Lemon Balm		

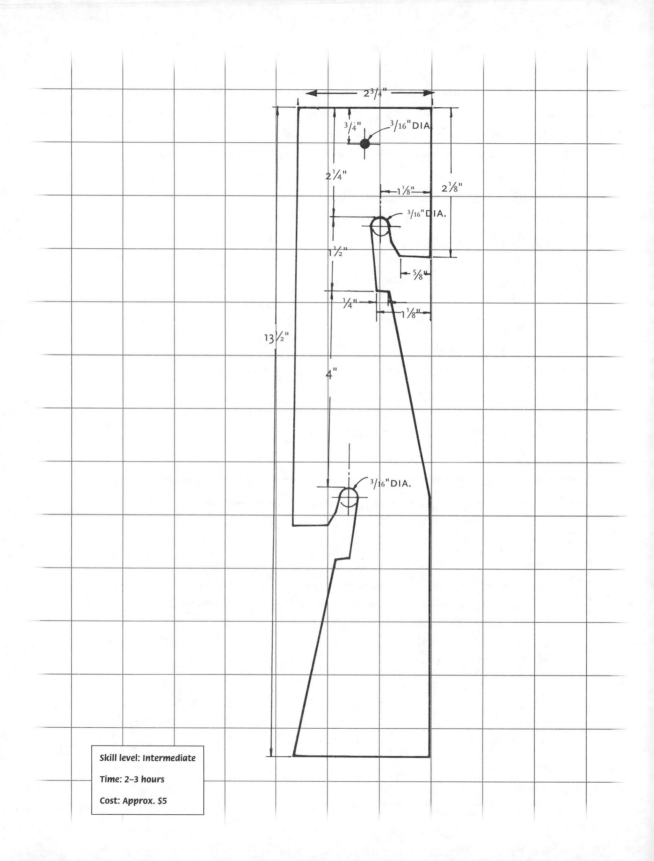

2³⁄₄"

³⁄₄"   ³⁄₁₆"DIA

2¹⁄₄"   1¹⁄₈"   2¹⁄₈"

³⁄₁₆"DIA.

1¹⁄₂"   ⁵⁄₈"

¹⁄₄"   1¹⁄₈"

13¹⁄₂"

4"

³⁄₁₆"DIA.

Skill level: Intermediate

Time: 2–3 hours

Cost: Approx. $5

Notched Pot Hanger

Design by Scott Banta

T HE SIMPLEST plant hangers are often the best. This hanger is an elegant solution for hanging two matching clay pots. The construction method is very easy and the combination of efficiency and sturdiness make this hanger an excellent choice for any room in the house. For a different look, paint the notched holder a bold solid color and the pots complementary colors, or paint the hanger and pots with the same faux finish for a seamless appearance. (See page 81 for how to create a japan finish.)

Materials

- One piece of hardwood, ¾" thick by 3" wide, 13" long
- Two terra-cotta pots
- One large eye screw
- Length of wire
- Wood stain or acrylic paint

Tools

- Handsaw
- Coping saw or keyhole saw
- Drill
- File or sandpaper
- Sliding bevel
- Paintbrush

Method

1. Cut the piece of wood to size.
2. Make a template for the notches as shown on the pattern.
3. Mark out the notches on the board. The notches on this pattern are 4" apart, but they could be placed 2½" to 3" apart.

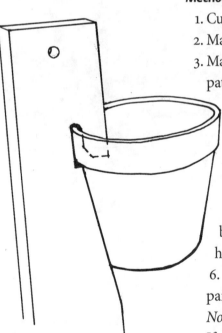

4. Drill a hole with a diameter the same as or greater than the thickness of the rim of the pot (in this case ³/16"). Use a saw to cut out the rest of the notch. Test the fit, filing or sanding as necessary. (Figure 16-1)

5. Drill a hole for the hook in the center top of the board. Attach a chain long enough to suspend the hanger at the desired height.

6. To finish the hanger, stain it or paint it with acrylic paint in the desired color and let it dry.

Note: This hanger can be lengthened to hold more pots. If more than two pot slots are built into the board, attach a bracket to the top to give it additional strength when hanging.

Figure 16-1

Japanning and Other Decorative Finishes for Wood

You can apply any number of treatments to the Notched Hanger. Paint the wood or stain it. For a sophisticated staining approach, apply faux wood inlay with wood stains. For a complete description of this technique, see Linda Buckingham and Leslie Bird's great book, *Projection Stenciling*.

Other options for decorating your Notched Hanger include stenciling, decoupage, sponging, and stamping. The Notched Pot Hanger is such a subtle, almost unnoticeable method of hanging pots that it can benefit from a dramatic decorative treatment.

If your pots are painted and finished to a high sheen, you may want to japan your wood hanger. Japanning developed as the European answer to Oriental lacquering. Chinese lacquering was a very labor-intensive and exacting method of producing a deep glossy finish on furniture. Japanning, which used materials available in Europe, was also time-consuming and, while not as perfect as true lacquering, still gave a sparkling and brilliant finish. Japanned pieces were painted with many layers of colored varnish, then had Asian-style designs applied, and finally, many coats of shellac, sanded between coats. If you want to try a simplified version of japanning on your Notched Pot Hanger, paint it with a solid coat of acrylic. Let it dry. Then paint it with at least four coats of tinted water-based varnish, allowing it to dry thoroughly between coats. Apply (either with a stencil or freehand) a design of your choosing in paint or pen. To truly get in the spirit of japanning, choose a design with an Asian flair (see the designs provided on page 51 for inspiration). Apply the same design to the pots that will be hung from the notches. Finally, paint the hanger with at least four coats of a water-based clear coat, allowing it to dry between coats. Your Notched Pot Hanger will be a lovely accent in the corner of a room.

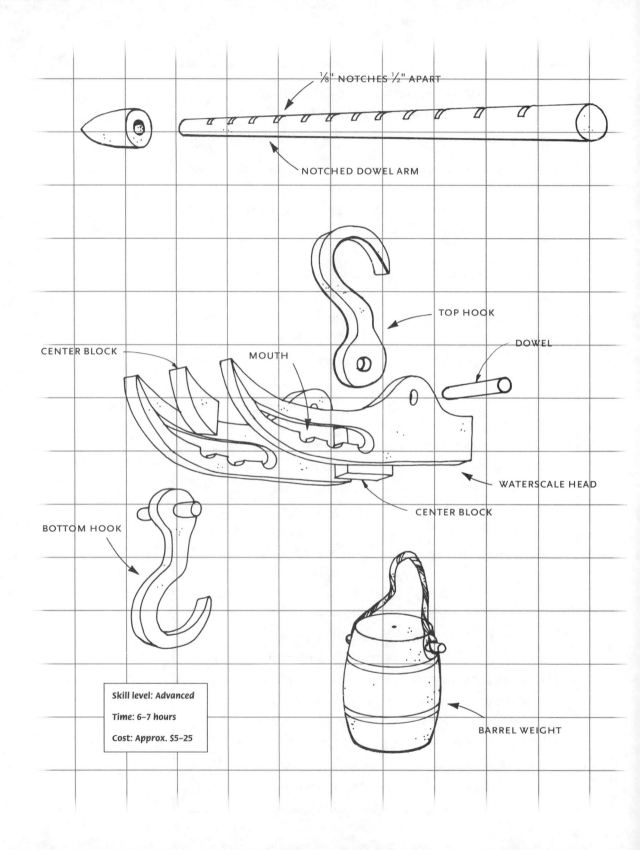

⅛" NOTCHES ½" APART

NOTCHED DOWEL ARM

TOP HOOK

DOWEL

CENTER BLOCK

MOUTH

WATERSCALE HEAD

BOTTOM HOOK

CENTER BLOCK

BARREL WEIGHT

Skill level: Advanced
Time: 6–7 hours
Cost: Approx. $5–25

Weighted Water Scale Hanger

SYD THOMSON is the designer of this attractive and useful plant hanger innovation. The weight and ballast system makes watering a breeze and the arrangement makes a lovely display in any corner. This hanger suspends a plant in my Aunt Terry's kitchen, where I have heard many people admire it. Try your hand at the design and wait for the intrigued responses.

Design by Syd Thomson

Materials

- Barrel weight (the one shown here is the common barrel weight found at hardware and lumber stores)
- A length of doweling for Notched Dowel Arm
- One block of wood
- One large piece of veneer to be cut and glued into layers to form the hook (you can also carve one from a solid piece of wood)
- Several small pieces of doweling for pins

Tools

- Chisel
- Saw
- Tape measure
- Pencil
- Sandpaper
- Carving knife
- Wood glue
- Bandsaw, fretsaw, or jigsaw

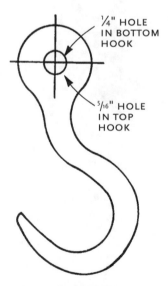

¼" HOLE IN BOTTOM HOOK

⁵⁄₁₆" HOLE IN TOP HOOK

Figure 17-1

Method

1. Using a saw, cut ⅛" deep notches at ½" intervals along one edge of a ⅜" diameter × 12" long hardwood dowel.
2. Use the pattern provided to cut two hooks from ¼" thick hardwood using a jigsaw, bandsaw, or fretsaw. Drill a ¼" diameter hole in one of the hooks as shown and glue in a ¼" diameter × ¾" long hardwood dowel. *Note:* Copy all patterns (Figures 17-1 to 17-3) at 133% on a photocopier to make them full size.
3. In the other hook, drill a ⁵⁄₁₆" diameter hole. *Note:* The hole in this hook must be larger than the hole in the other to allow this one to freely rotate around a ¼" dowel.
4. To make the "head" of the waterscale, use the pattern provided and cut two side pieces from ¼" thick hardwood.

Drill a ¼" diameter hole as shown in the pattern, and drill four ⁵⁄₁₆" diameter holes in the "mouth" before sawing it out with a fretsaw. *Note:* The sawblade enters and exits the mouth at this point (Figure 17-2).

5. Using the pattern for the head, saw out two center blocks from ⁵⁄₁₆" thick hardwood.

6. Glue all four pieces together as shown on page 78, being sure to put the upper and lower hooks in place beforehand. (Glue a ¼" diameter dowel in place in the head for the upper hook to rotate on).

7. Drill a ⅜" diameter hole into the top of the head and glue one end of the dowel into it. *Note:* Be sure the notches on the dowel are facing up!

8. You can turn the knob at the other end of the dowel on a lathe (Figure 17-3) or take the pattern to a craft or lumber supply store and but a suitable dowel. Any interesting wood knob will work. Drill a ⅜" diameter hole into the knob and glue it in place over the other end of the dowel.

9. The 3½" high wood barrel weight was turned on a lathe, but you may purchase something similar at a craft or lumber supply shop. Drill a ¼" diameter hole near the top of the barrel for a dowel of the same size. Attach a cord to either end of this dowel as shown on page 82.

10. Sand each of the pieces and finish with furniture oil, wax, varnish, or paint.

11. Hang a pot from the bottom hook and the barrel from the dowel arm. Suspend the waterscale hanger from the top hook and adjust the weight along the arm until the scale hangs even. When your plant needs water you will find the weight moves down and the pot moves up. This is a great hanger for neglectful gardeners and those who dislike plunging fingers into soil to test for moisture!

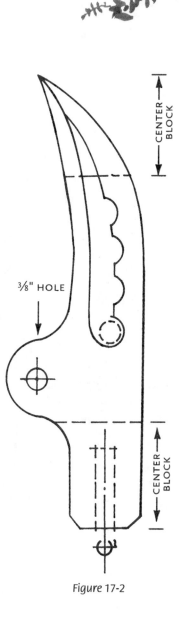

⅜" HOLE

Figure 17-2

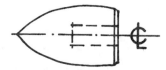

Figure 17-3

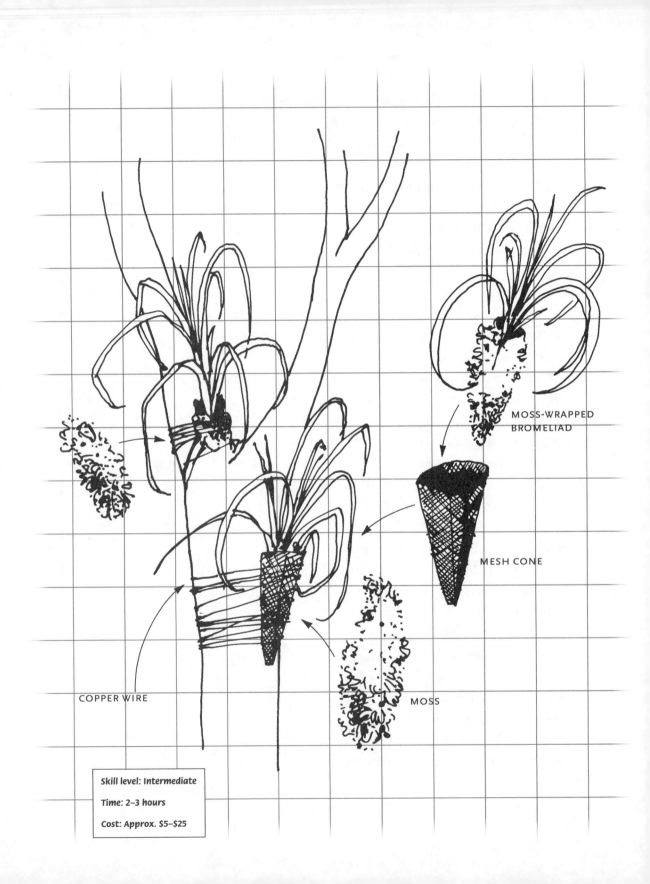

MOSS-WRAPPED
BROMELIAD

MESH CONE

COPPER WIRE

MOSS

Skill level: Intermediate

Time: 2–3 hours

Cost: Approx. $5–$25

Epiphyte Branch

T HE EPIPHYTE BRANCH will be
a showpiece in a plant window. It is
simply a bark-covered branch planted
with epiphytic plants, which are those that
don't require soil and instead grow on trees
or rocks. They are also called air plants.

You can hang your branch in a plant
window or, for a more natural appearance,
place it upright in your plant window.
Stand it up in a large container filled with
wet concrete or plaster of paris. Support
the branch while it dries and then plant it with
epiphytes. Choose the hardest wood you can find for your epiphyte branch, as it will have to withstand a lot of humidity. You
will probably need to replace the branch every few years. Also,
try to find natural deadfall rather than cutting portions off a
healthy tree.

Bromeliads and orchids are two important types of plants

suitable for an epiphyte branch. Epiphytes use their elevated location get more exposure to sunlight. They come from tropical regions and tend to require high humidity. To fasten your epiphytes to your branch, wrap them in damp sphagnum moss and then tie the bundle to the branch with thin copper wire, or fashion small wire baskets and plant them with moss and epiphytes. Epiphytes can also be attached to pieces of tree fern fibre, bark, or cork and covered in osmunda. Wind the roots of your epiphyte around the supports and cover them with damp moss. Epiphytes appreciate infrequent applications of liquid fertilizer.

Some Popular Epiphytes

Aechmea fasciata
Aerides crassifolium
Aerides odoratum
Asplenium bulbiferum
Billbergia 'Fantasia'
Brassavola digbyana
Brassaia maculata
Bromelia balansae
Bulbophyllum lobbii
Captosis berteroniana
Captosis floribunda

Cirrhopetalum cumingi
Davallia bullata mariesii
Epiphyllum hybrids
Guzmania lingulata
Hatiora salicorniorides
Neoreglia carolinae
Philodendron bipinnatifidum
Platycerium bifurcatum
Platyclinis filiformus
Tillandsia ionanthe
Vriesea malzinei

Plant Windows

The ultimate indoor plant place, a well-planned and executed plant window will serve in place of blinds and curtains. Plants in a plant window must be able to withstand bright light and you won't be able to open your window, but the visual impact is unparalleled.

The simplest method of creating a plant window is to buy or

make a series of glass shelves and either place them on a ledge in front of a window or build them right into the window frame. Such shelves make great display places for collections of cacti and succulents.

Traditional plant windows are classed as either open or closed. Closed plant windows are essentially greenhouses built right into the window frame. They require a great deal of attention and are difficult to build in a window that has not been designed with that purpose in mind. Open plant windows are so called because there is no glass separating the plants from the interior of the room. Open plant windows require some construction and preparation to ensure the comfort of the plants that will live in it, but are still much easier to create than a closed plant window.

To make an open plant window, you will need to make sure the window is not drafty and that the window ledge is wide enough to hold a collection of potted plants in tubs. If you have a heater under the window, or a draft, a styrofoam mat on the windowsill will help prevent extremes of air temperature from injuring the plants. The plant tubs or boxes should be filled with volcanic rock or broken pieces of clay and kept moist to increase humidity in the window. Combine hanging plants and epiphyte branches to cover the entire window.

Bamboo and wood slat boxes are ideal for hanging plants in windows (See Project 14 for a Bamboo Orchid Basket) and these can be hung from the ceiling or from an epiphyte branch, which is the centerpiece of most plant windows.

Glass Window Shelves

You can easily add glass shelves across the length of a window by adding strips of molding on either side of the frame as supports for glass shelves.

Have a glazier cut and sand the edges of ½" glass shelves that measure ½" less than the width of the window frame. The moldings should be cut (two on either side) to the same depth as the window frame.

Glass shelves work best in deep windows that receive a lot of light.

Part Two

Boxes and Baskets

Boxes and Baskets

VOLUMES HAVE been written about the art of planting window boxes and baskets. Less information is available on building your own baskets and boxes. In this section you will find a variety of basic projects for creating your own displays.

Scale, materials, and your choice of plants all contribute to the overall appearance of your boxes or baskets. For instance, if you choose a selection of small baskets, paint them white, and use them to hold a combination of miniature roses and baby's breath, and place them on a whitewashed dresser, the effect will be delicate and pretty. If you build the Twig and Vine Planter, plant it with pansies, ivy, and sage surrounded by moss, and place it on the windowsill of your cottage, the effect will be rustic and robust.

Choose plants that fit the season and the look of the box or basket. For instance, the Driftwood Basket is the perfect home for a selection of perennial wild grasses in colors from black to silver. The driftwood shaped by time and the sea complements the natural grace of the grasses, bent but unbreaking in the wind. The Wall-Mounted Plant Box, on the other hand, is a very polished project for the intermediate to advanced woodworker. The box has a structural elegance, and indoor gardeners will appreciate the innovative design that enables them to lift it on and off the wall when it is time to perform maintenance on the plants. The Wall-Mounted Plant Box suits special plants, such as orchids or bonsai or any indoor plants with interesting shapes.

When planting window boxes, try to vary the heights of the plants. The traditional shape of the window box is tall plants to the back, shorter plants in front. Trailers such as ivy at the corners and in front will give your boxes a fluid, rampant look. Choose plants that suit one another, such as those that originate in the same area and require the same growing conditions. It isn't necessary to plant boxes so that they are perfectly symmetrical. Nature is irregular and profuse and can be interpreted beautifully in a window box or basket. If you want a very formal planting, choose a traditional plant that you can shape to emphasize the formal look of the basket.

Before planting your window box or basket, decide if you want to use it indoors or out. If it is going to live outdoors, determine whether if you want it to weather naturally. If not, protect it with a weatherproofing treatment. Naturally weathered baskets and boxes look wonderfully at home in the garden, but protective treatment will extend your planter's life.

Seasonal Window Boxes

Fall Box
Hardy chrysanthemums
Blue trailing campanula
Pink cyclamen
Dark green hebe
(Plant in July for a peak display in October.)

Summer Boxes
White snapdragons
Pink geraniums
Pink impatiens
White and blue lobelia
Variegated ivy

White geraniums
White marguerites
White bacopa
White trailing verbena
Yellow petunias

(Plant in mid-May for a peak display all summer long.)

Spring Box
Salmon tulips
Small white hyacinths
White winter pansies
Kale
(Plant in September for a constant flowering display throughout the winter.)

Winter Boxes
Partridgeberry (Winterberry)
Bugle *(Ajuga reptans)*
Mahonia japonica
Variegated periwinkle
Dwarf daffodils
Snowdrops
Variegated ivy
Purple crocuses

Huechera 'Rachel'

Gaulthiera procumbens
Erica gracilis
Carex conica
Juniperus horizontalis

(Plant in September for handsome displays year-round.)

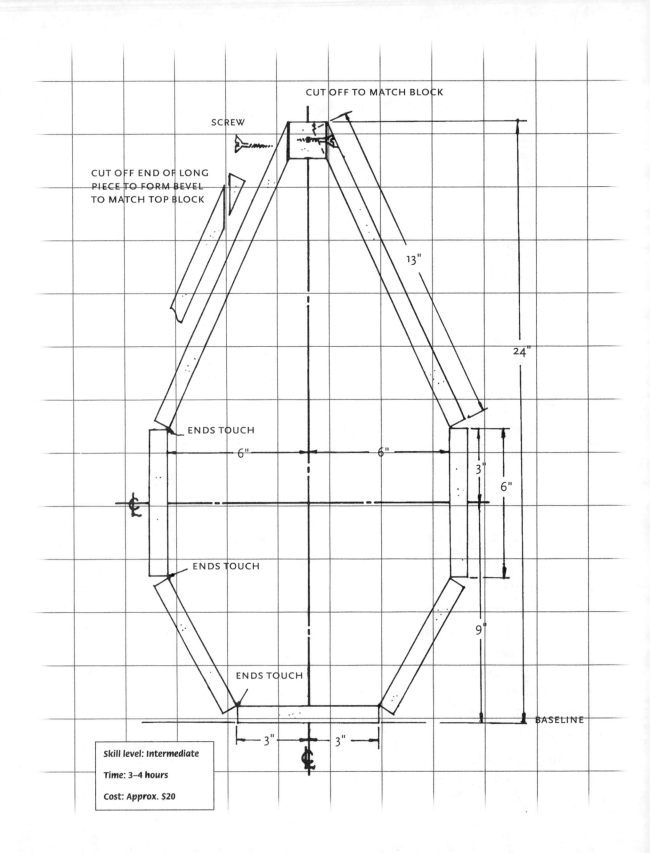

CUT OFF TO MATCH BLOCK

SCREW

CUT OFF END OF LONG
PIECE TO FORM BEVEL
TO MATCH TOP BLOCK

13"

24"

ENDS TOUCH

6"   6"

3"

6"

ENDS TOUCH

9"

ENDS TOUCH

BASELINE

3"   3"

Skill level: Intermediate

Time: 3–4 hours

Cost: Approx. $20

Wood Block Basket

Design by Scott Banta

THIS WOOD BLOCK basket can be hung or stood on a table or shelf. Use it indoors or outdoors to carry produce in from the garden or to show off large ivy spilling out the sides and trailing up the handles. Unique and simple enough for anyone to construct, the basket can help you to use up extra pieces of wood around the shop. Try cedar blocks to give your basket a warm hue that will make any plant look wonderful. The woodworker hidden in all of us can rejoice in the simplicity of this basket.

95

Materials

- (D) Seventy-two pieces of 6" × ¾" × ¾" wood such as western red cedar (Use scrap pieces or get lengths of wood from a lumber store and cut them on a tablesaw or with a handsaw. You might also try the generosity of a carpenter friend for cutting the wood into pieces.)
- (A) Five pieces of 6" × 1½" × ¾" wood
- (B) Two pieces of 13½" × 1½" × ¾" wood
- (C) One piece of 1½" × 1½" × 1½" wood
- Water-resistant wood glue such as Type II PVA
- At least ½ - lb. 1¼" galvanized nails
- A sheet of plain paper at least 25" × 15"
- Sanding sealer
- 220 grit garnet paper
- Exterior varnish with UV protection (if you plan to use the planter outside)

Tools

- Hammer
- Small handsaw
- Safety glasses
- Workbench or plywood work surface
- Tape
- Ruler

Method

1. Tape your sheet of paper to a workbench or plywood work surface and draw a vertical center line with your ruler from the top to the bottom of the paper (or simply fold the paper in half).
2. At least 9" from the bottom of the paper, draw a horizontal center line perpendicular to the vertical line. These will be your work baselines (Figure 19-1).
3. For the first layer of the planter, arrange the seven ¾" × 1½"

pieces (A) on the edge (as shown in Figure 19-2). Place two 6" pieces approximately 1' apart, parallel to the centerline and each about 6" from it with their centers about 9" from the base. Place the two remaining 6" long pieces at angles on either side of the bottom piece until all five pieces touch (Figure 19-2). The 1½" cube (C) is centered at the top and the two 13½" long pieces (B) are placed on either side. The acute angles at the top are marked and cut to fit tight to either side of the 1½" cube. Glue and nail the cube in place as shown.

4. For Layer Two, all of the remaining pieces are ¾" square and 6" long (D). At the center of the bottom piece, place the first two of the eight pieces that make up this layer at angles determined by where their corners meet the inside edge of the first layer (as shown in Figure 19-3). Glue and nail these pieces in place and then continue in a like manner with three more pieces on either side. With the piece nailed together, turn it over and repeat the second layer on the other side.

5. Layer Three has seven pieces. The first one is placed at the bottom, parallel to the bottom piece of the first layer and centered on the vertical center line 2" up from the bottom. Finish off this layer like the previous one, and turn it over again to repeat Layer Three on the opposite side.

6. Layer Four uses six pieces and is applied like Layer Two on both sides.

7. Layer Five uses five pieces and is applied like Layer Three on both sides.

8. Layer Six is a repeat of Layer Two.

9. Layer Seven is a repeat of Layer Five.

10. Layer Eight is another repeat of Layer Two.

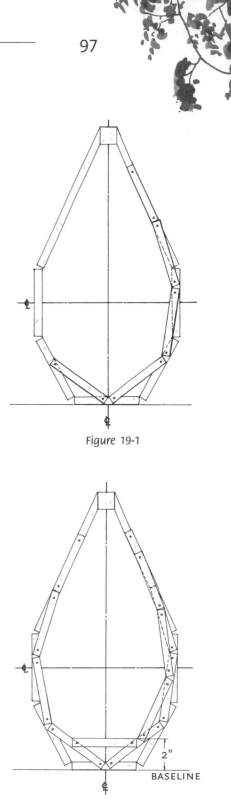

Figure 19-1

Figure 19-2

11. Layer Nine uses only one piece laid parallel to all of the other bottom pieces (Figure 19-5).

12. To finish the wood block basket, apply one coat of sanding sealer. Brush it on and around all of the pieces, followed by a light sanding with #220 grit sandpaper. Finally, if you intend to use the basket outdoors, apply two coats of exterior varnish, allowing the first coat to dry before the next is applied.

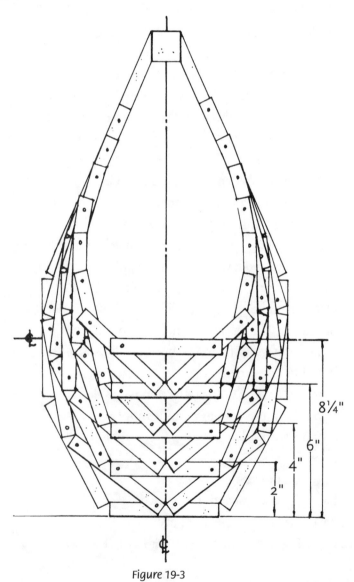

Figure 19-3

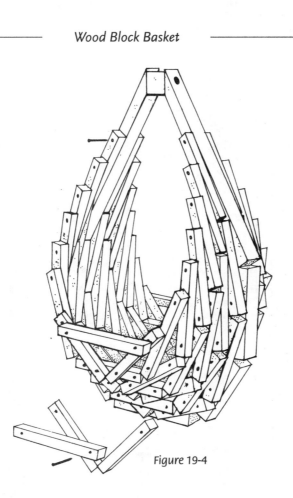

Figure 19-4

Plant Ideas

The Wood Block Basket makes a wonderful outdoor setting for a combination of red nasturtiums and marigold "Lemon Gem" or pink begonia, blue lobelia, and silver nettle vine. For these plantings, line the bottoms and the sides of the basket with a fine mesh screen or moss, and fill it almost to the top with outdoor potting soil. Keep the smaller plants such as marigolds at the sides and the taller plants in the center. Hang the basket with a secure hook or sit it on a rustic wood block pedestal made with weathered cedar.

Other useful and attractive combinations for the Wood Block Basket include violas and parsley, dwarf tomatoes, small marigolds and basil, or green peppers, marigolds and parsley.

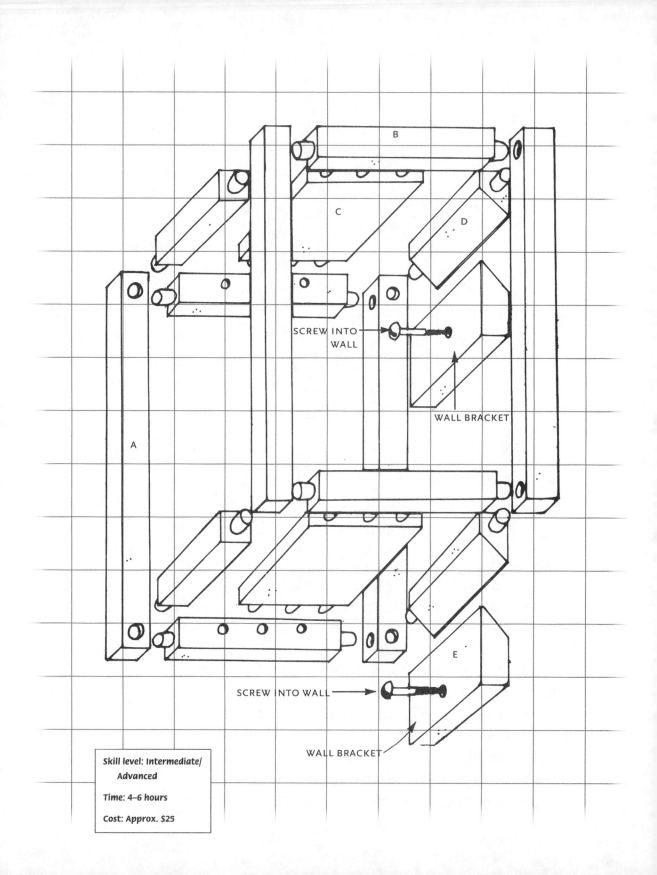

B

C

D

SCREW INTO
WALL

WALL BRACKET

A

E

SCREW INTO WALL

WALL BRACKET

Skill level: Intermediate/
Advanced

Time: 4–6 hours

Cost: Approx. $25

Wall-Mounted Plant Box

Design by Scott Banta

Tʜɪꜱ ɪɴɴᴏᴠᴀᴛɪᴠᴇ, attractive, and handy hanging plant box will be the answer to many an indoor gardener's wishes. Its subtle structural grace will complement any décor and make looking after your plants simple. You can slide it on and off its wall supports when you need to tend or adjust the plants. Holding one or two potted plants, it can be a showcase or a lovely accent.

Materials

Frame:

- (A) Four 17" × 1¼" square pieces of wood
- (B) Six 7" × 1¼" square pieces of wood
- (C) Two 7" × 4½" × ½" pieces of wood
- (D) Two 7" × 2" × 1¼" pieces of wood

Support Pieces:

- (E) Two 7" × 1¼" × 2" pieces of wood
- #8 roundhead screws
- White or yellow carpenter's glue

  Note: If your lumberyard doesn't carry 1¼" square pine, fir, or cedar for this box and its supports, you can buy it in 4' lengths, 1½" square. This 1½" square lumber can then be planed down 1¼" square and cut to the required lengths with a handsaw. The place at which you buy your lumber should be willing to plane it for you. Another option is to rip the pieces from a wide board using a tablesaw and then cut them to length.

Tools

- Crosscut handsaw or tablesaw
- Drill with ¼" and ½" bits
- Dowel centering points
- Bar or pipe clamps

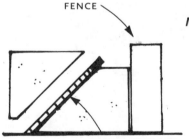

FENCE

TABLESAW BLADE

Figure 20-1

Method

1. Before you begin, look carefully at the diagram on page 100, the exploded view. Cut all the 1¼" stock to the required lengths.

2. Cut a 45° angle on one side of each of the four 1¼" × 2" pieces (D and E). The angle does not have to be exact, as long as they are all the same. A tablesaw is ideal for achieving even angles (Figure 20-1).

3. Drill ½" diameter dowel holes ⅝" deep in each 1¼" square × 17" long piece, as well as two of the pieces with an angle along one edge (B and D).

4. Using ½" diameter dowel-centering points, locate corresponding dowel holes in the sides of the four 1¼" square × 17" pieces (A) (Figure 20-2).

5. Repeat this process with the two ½" thick pieces with three ¼" diameter dowels at each end (C).

6. With all the dowels in place, assemble the frame without glue to be sure it will fit together easily and accurately. You can make small adjustments by enlarging holes and/or sanding dowels if necessary. The glue can also fill in small gaps.

7. Once you are satisfied it will fit together tightly with square corners all around, put a drop of glue in each hole, insert the dowels, and clamp the two opposite sides (Figure 20-3).

8. When the glue has dried, glue and clamp the two remaining pieces to complete the sides of the box.

9. The two supports must be screwed directly through the wallboard into a stud to make sure the weight of the box and two plants is secure. Locate a stud with a hammer or electronic stud finder. Through the center of each support, drill a hole to match the diameter of the screw.

   Screw the upper support into place first, and then hang the plant box on it to exactly locate the position of the lower one. Mark that position on the wall, remove the plant box, and then screw the lower support in place.

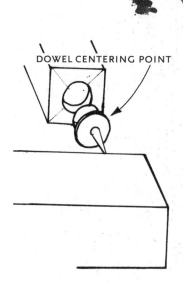

DOWEL CENTERING POINT

Figure 20-2

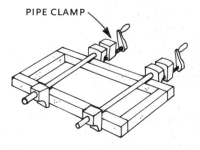

PIPE CLAMP

Figure 20-3

Version with Tenons

If you would like to build the Wall-Mounted Plant Box using a more sophisticated building method, try making a version that uses tenons rather than dowels. To make mortise and tenon joints, add an inch to all the 7" long pieces (making them 8") to allow for a ½" tenon on each end (Figure 20-4). With a ¾" diameter drill bit and a sharp ½" wide chisel, cut ½" deep mortises in the 17" long pieces.

Note: Experiment with size, form, and textural differences on the different levels, with plants such as lipstick plant, asparagus fern, baby's tears, and bromeliads (see list on page 105 for more suggestions).

Figure 20-4

Another Option for the Wall-Mounting Method

The unique removable wall-mounting method will also work for shelves. To make a wall-mounted shelf follow the directions below.

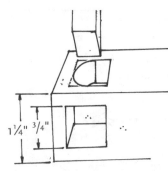

Figure 20-5

Materials

Support Piece:
- (D) One 7" × 1½" piece
- Two #8 roundhead screws

Shelf:
- (A) One 9" × 10" × ½" peice
- (B) Two 8" × 10" × ½" pieces
- (C) One 7" × 1½" piece
- ¼" diameter dowels or #10 flathead screws
- White glue

Tools
- Jigsaw
- Electric drill
- Screwdriver

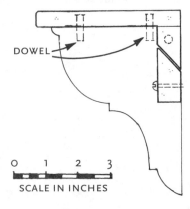

Figure 20-6

Method

1. Enlarge the pattern provided to full size on a photocopier.
2. Cut out sides (B) using a jigsaw or bandsaw.
3. Round the front corners (1" radius) with a bandsaw and sandpaper.
4. Cut the angles on pieces (C) and (D) as described in step 2 on page 102.
5. Assemble the four parts of the shelf with glue and dowels.
6. Sand and finish the shelves with oil, stain, or paint.

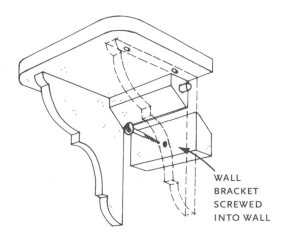

WALL BRACKET SCREWED INTO WALL

Figure 20-7

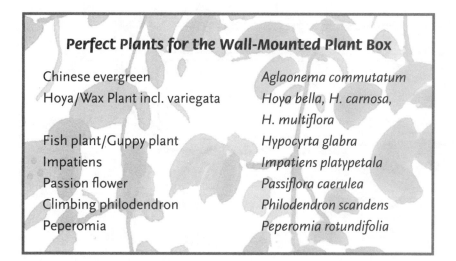

Perfect Plants for the Wall-Mounted Plant Box

Chinese evergreen	*Aglaonema commutatum*
Hoya/Wax Plant incl. variegata	*Hoya bella, H. carnosa, H. multiflora*
Fish plant/Guppy plant	*Hypocyrta glabra*
Impatiens	*Impatiens platypetala*
Passion flower	*Passiflora caerulea*
Climbing philodendron	*Philodendron scandens*
Peperomia	*Peperomia rotundifolia*

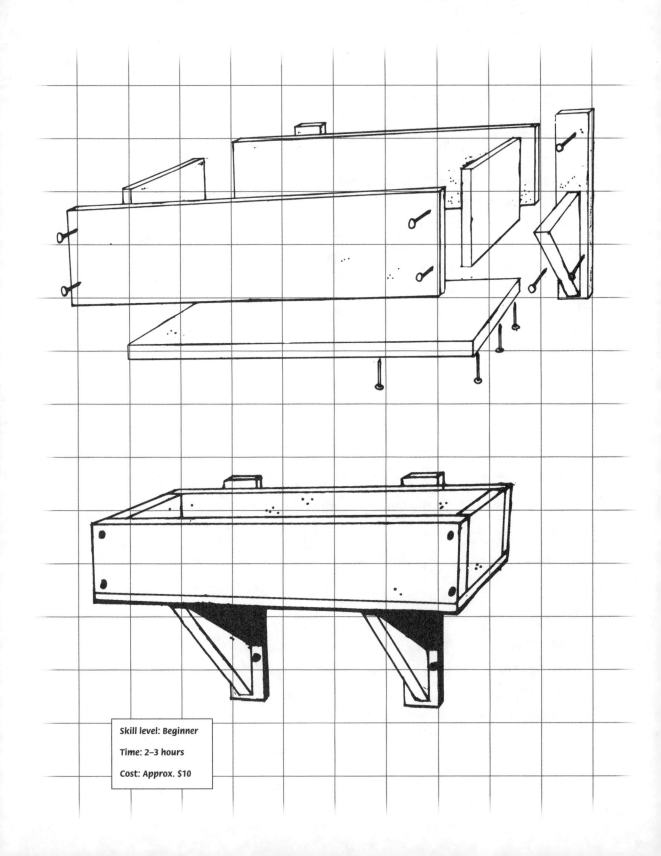

Skill level: Beginner

Time: 2–3 hours

Cost: Approx. $10

Project 21

Rustic Window Box

Design by Scott Banta

THIS IS WOODWORKING made easy in a project that almost anyone with a few basic tools can construct. One of the beauties of plants is that they can be shown to advantage in settings that range from rustic, like this window box, to very sophisticated. This simple box is perfect for a display of cheerful nodding pansies or a winter showcase of colored grasses, wintergreen, and heather.

Materials

- Any lumber 1" × 6" or larger (recycled cedar siding, as used here, is ideal)
- Two 1" × 8" sides and a 1" × 10" bottom (will provide a depth of 7½")
- One 10" × 10" board for supports
- Nails

Tools

- Handsaw (or tablesaw)
- Hammer

Method

1. Cut the sides and bottom to length (your local lumberyard or friendly woodworker may be willing to cut these pieces for you if you don't have a tablesaw or the energy to cut the pieces by hand).
2. Nail the sides to the bottom.
3. Cut the ends to fit, making sure that the grain is horizontal. This construction will ensure that the wood can move without creating gaps.
4. Nail the ends in place.
5. Cut a 10" × 10" board in half diagonally and secure it to the bottom. You can also buy supports to fit under the box. *Note:* You can leave the box on the ground, keeping in mind that it should be raised off the ground at least 1" or so to allow air to move under it and to keep pests and mildew from accumulating underneath. This is true of all planters kept on the ground. Small wooden slats are a simple way to raise containers off the ground.
6. You can leave the box natural, stain it, or paint it.

Liners for Baskets and Boxes

Cardboard Liners (whalehide liners)
Made to fit particular baskets. Plants can be inserted into slits in the sides.

Cellulose Fiber Liners (recycled)
These are designed to fit with particular wire baskets and are not transferable to other uses.

Coir Fiber Liners (or coconut mat)
These liners made of coconut and jute last for more than one season, but can be tricky to plant through when placed in a basket.

Polyethylene
These liners are inexpensive and unobtrusive when the plants are all grown in, but can be a bit of an eyesore when the plantings are new and the liner shows through the basket or open-sided box.

Polyurethane Foam
These are inexpensive, last well, and are easy to plant through.

Sphagnum Moss
This is the traditional favorite, but to be kept green it must be watered frequently. Another drawback is the cost of fresh moss.

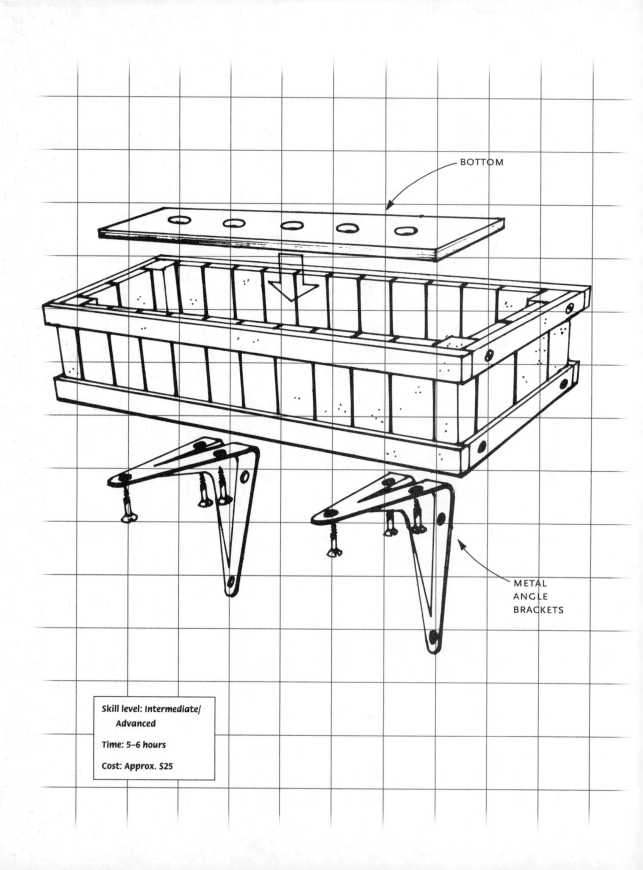

BOTTOM

METAL
ANGLE
BRACKETS

Skill level: Intermediate/
Advanced

Time: 5–6 hours

Cost: Approx. $25

Project 22

Edged Window Box

Design by Scott Banta

THIS HANDSOME box is a more challenging and polished-looking project than the Rustic Window Box and it takes slightly more skill to construct. The end result is a lovely wooden box for your plants and flowers. This box will look good in any number of locations, particularly wood patios.

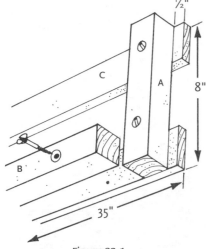

Figure 22-1

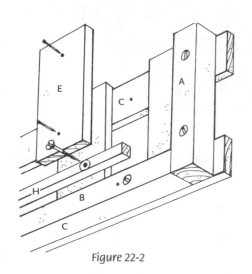

Figure 22-2

Materials

- (A) Four 8" × 1½" × 1½" pieces of wood (any wood will work, but cedar ages particularly well)
- (B) Two 31" × 1½" × 1½" pieces
- (C) Four 35" × 2" × ½" pieces
- (D) Four 8" × 2" × ½" pieces
- (E) Twenty-five 6½" × 4" × ½" pieces
- (F) Two 5" × 1½" × 1½" pieces
- (G) Four 6½" × 2½" × ½" pieces
- (H) Two 30" × ¾" × ¾" pieces
- (I) One 30¾" × 5½" × ½" piece of plywood (or ¾")
- Eight 1¼" screws
- Twenty-six 1¾" screws
- Six ⅝" flathead screws
- Waterproof glue

Tools

- Tablesaw
- Drill and a selection of bits
- Hammer
- ⅞" nails

Method

1. Screw and glue one (A) piece to each end of both (B)s, using four 2½" screws. Predrill the holes with a 3/32" bit and countersink.
2. To make the sides, screw two (C)s to each assembly, flush with the top and bottom, overhanging an even ½" on both ends, using six 1¾" screws (Figure 22-1).
3. Nail the (E)s to the inside of the (C) pieces using ⅞" nails (Figure 22-2). Because 4" does not divide into 31", the final piece must be custom cut to 2¾".

Do not glue these pieces. Instead nail them with slight gaps between them, to allow for swelling and movement in the wood.

4. Screw and glue one (H) piece to each (B), keeping them flush with the bottom. This will support the bottom.

5. Screw and glue the (F) pieces to the (D) pieces, centered lengthwise and flush with the bottom edge using four 1¾" screws.

6. To make the ends, nail and glue two (G) pieces to each (D) piece, resting on (F) and flush with its ends.

7. Nail another (D) piece to the top of the (G)s, making a short version of the sides.

8. Glue and screw the two end panels to the (A) pieces of both long sides to form the box (Figure 22-4).

9. Cut plywood for the bottom and drill five or six ¼" holes for drainage.

10. Paint or stain the box as desired, then assemble.

11. Hang the box using commercial bracket supports or build supports like those used in the Rustic Window Box shown on page 106.

12. If you want to adjust the box so it is more than 2½' long, supports are a good idea. In that case, space them 16" apart, so they can be screwed into wall studs.

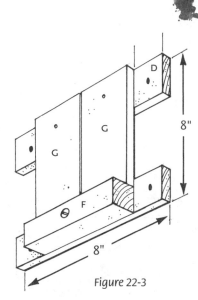

Figure 22-3

Plant Ideas

If you have a bright spot to locate your box, combine white and mauve lobelias, variegated ivy, white and pink impatiens, and mauve and purple geraniums.

This box would also be ideal for planting a combination of "Tumbler" tomatoes, chives, parsley, chamomile, lemon balm, and nasturtiums.

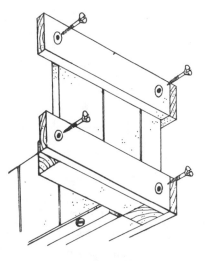

Figure 22-4

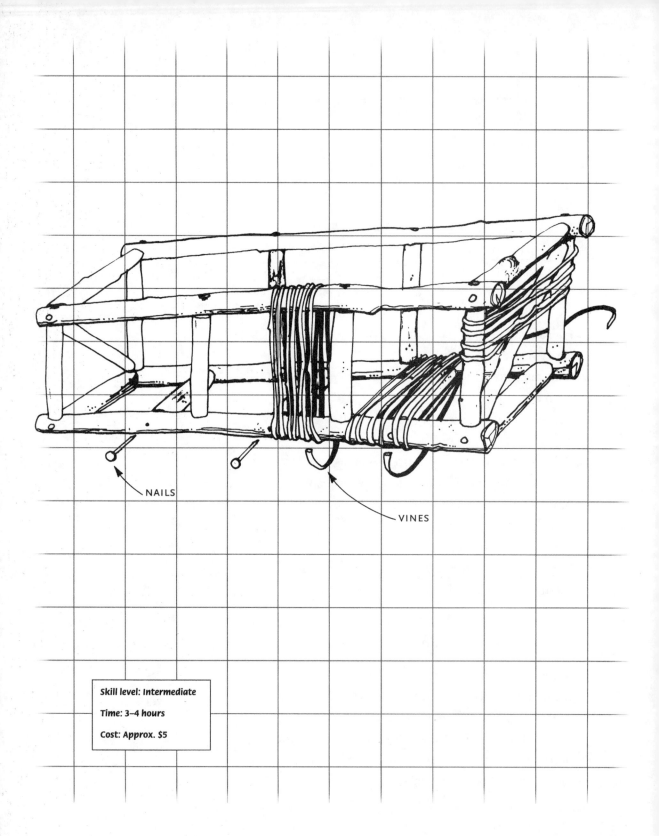

NAILS

VINES

Skill level: *Intermediate*

Time: *3–4 hours*

Cost: *Approx. $5*

Wooden Plant Tables

These plant tables are inspired by the classic lines of traditional Japanese furniture.

The proportions are elegant and reflect the influence of a tradition based on admiration for wood and the art of woodworking.

This pair of matched tables will be a rewarding project for novice to advanced woodworkers and a stylish place to display a variety of plants in pots of different sizes.

Crocheted Wire Plant Bag

A crocheted wire bag makes a wonderful disguise for a bland pot.

This bag combines silver, aqua, and red wire, for a bright and sparkling effect that works perfectly with succulents and other hanging desert dwellers.

The bag has crocheted wires which run up the built-in arms of the hanger for decorative effect.

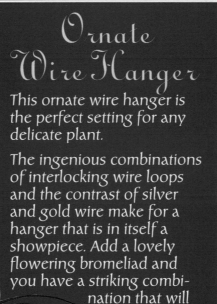

Ornate Wire Hanger

This ornate wire hanger is the perfect setting for any delicate plant.

The ingenious combinations of interlocking wire loops and the contrast of silver and gold wire make for a hanger that is in itself a showpiece. Add a lovely flowering bromeliad and you have a striking combination that will lend interest and beauty to any corner.

Twig and Vine Planter

The twig and vine box is a wonderful planter in the finest rustic tradition.

The natural beauty and simplicity of the twig and vine construction perfectly complements a variety of plantings. Simple to construct and timeless in its style, this box will enhance any porch, window ledge, or garden pathway.

Copper Trio

Copper is the perfect metal to show off plants. These succulents are set off beautifully by their glinting copper containers and hangers.

The punched copper hanger fastened with brass wire holding a clay pot, the delicate woven copper container holding the verdigris painted pot, and the woven brass and copper hanger all show off their hardy little inhabitants perfectly.

Playful Piñata
&
Santa Fé Hanger

Buy a piñata or make one from scratch to hold a cactus collection in a child's room.

Use traditional knotwork and Southwestern motifs to hang a trio of tiny cacti pots.

Sculptural Statements

Here dyed green bamboo has been fashioned into a lovely teepee trellis wrapped with wire and raffia (left), and a simple and ingenious three-legged plant stand (right). Inexpensive and easy to find, bamboo can be the best friend of both the indoor and the outdoor gardener.

Raffia-covered wire adds to the tropical feel of the bamboo plant stand and to the elegance of the trellis. Both the stand and the trellis are suitable for use inside or out-doors with a wide assortment of plants. Use these creations as permanent or temporary show-cases for special plants.

Wood Basket

The rich red of the cedar blocks that make up this basket will enhance any planting.

The basket can be hung or stood on a table or ledge, and used indoors or out. Use the wood block basket to carry that bumper crop of carrots or an extravagant armful of sweet peas from the garden.

Terracotta
Pot Finishes

Terra-cotta is the perfect surface for faux finishes. A pot painted a rich red and edged with metallic gold is an elegant home for miniature roses.

Stenciling, crackling, and decoupage take clay pots to another level. Faux finishes will help you transform simple pots into wonderful accents for the home.

Here you see a wood ring hanger painted and decoupaged to match a pot, a burgundy pot covered in fantastic card art, and a pot under-painted green, topped with a crackled eggshell coat, and finished with gold accents and a stenciled beetle.

Lacy Wire Fern Hanger

Traditional Victorian fern hangers were showpieces made of splendidly ornate wrought iron.

Using chicken wire, silver wire, and decorative chain you can reinterpret the intricate beauty of the antique originals.

Terrific Topiary

Many gardeners love to shape nature to their own designs. Let your playful and creative side show by creating an unusual topiary.

The chicken shown here is shaped and supported with a galvanized wire frame. Its beak is made with a cone-shaped piece of hardware cloth (wire mesh).

The monkey is a chicken wire form stuffed with ivy, and hung on a driftwood trellis. Suspended in a tree, he drew gasps of delight from startled visitors.

Creating topiaries will bring out the artist and the dreamer in you.

Natural Beauties

Red cedar is a wonderfully attractive material for window boxes. It weathers well and, if left unfinished, will take on a delicate silvery hue. Treated with a weather-resistant finish, cedar window boxes will maintain their beautiful golden-red color.

Harmony and Balance

This collection of hangers, baskets, and planters shows the range of inexpensive and innovative materials you can use to house your plants.

Glass, driftwood, rusted metal, concrete, and brass enhance one another and show off an assortment of lovely plants.

Project 23

Twig and Vine Planter

Design by Scott Banta

THIS RUSTIC twig planter is the ideal setting for a rampant and wild display. Lined with rich green moss, the planter will be a showpiece in your garden, along a path, on a porch, or outside a front gate. You will also have the pleasure of gathering your building materials in the woods and getting in the mood for a bit of gardening.

Materials

- Four 10" twigs, approximately ¾" in diameter (willow twigs were used for this planter)
- Four 32" twigs, approximately 1" in diameter
- Twelve 9½" twigs, ¾" in diameter. Cut these as you need them and custom fit (approximately 30'–40').
- Enough vine to wrap the sides and bottom of the entire box. Any flexible vine such as hops or grape will work.
- Thirty #6 screws
- Wood glue (optional)
- Enough moss to line the back and bottom. Moss is available at most garden centers and plant nurseries.
- *Optional:* If you want to hang the twig box, you can use regular steel shelf supports 8"–10" or a decorative bracket .

Tools

- Small saw for cutting twigs
- Clippers or heavy-duty scissors for cutting vine
- Drill (electric or hand) and #2 Robertson or Phillips bit
- Work gloves
- Safety glasses
- Knife or chisel for making bark flaps
- Stapler

Method

1. To begin, find and cut the twigs and vine as needed and bring them back to your work space. Cut the long pieces to length first. The cross pieces are best cut to fit as you build.
2. Build the basic frame. You can hide the screws by cutting a flap of bark where the screw is intended to go, lifting it, inserting the screw, and then gluing the bark flap back down.
3. Determine spacing of the cross pieces; 3"–4" spacing is usually best.

4. Measure and cut each piece to allow for irregularities in the long pieces.

5. Once all the pieces are screwed into place, begin wrapping the vine. Wrap the vine as tightly as possible, cinching the ends under the previous wrap, and stapling where necessary.

6. To line the planter with moss, stuff the space between the vines from the inside. Start at the bottom and work up, packing the moss firmly in place. Use the largest pieces of moss to create an even layer on the sides. Coconut mat or another manufactured layering product could also be used inside the planter in a single layer. You might also consider building the box around a plastic liner, and adjusting the measurements to fit.

Plant suggestions

This box, lined with moss, suits any wild-looking flowers or foliage. Ivy, silver nettle, nasturtium, petunia, bidens, weigela, begonia, or helichrysum are just a few of the possibilities.

Suggested Combinations
Geraniums, silver nettle vine, lobelia
Impatiens, bacopa, verbena

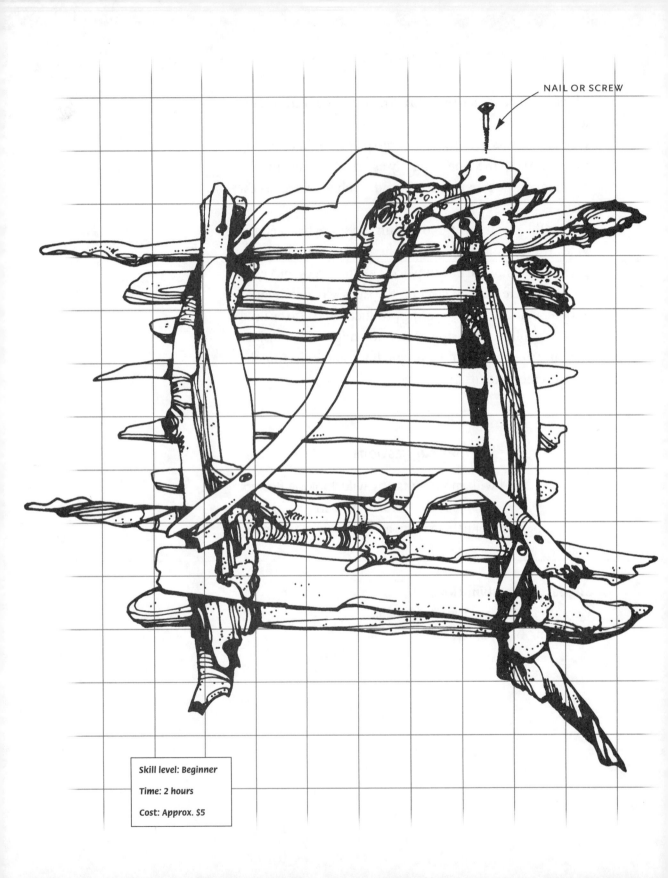

NAIL OR SCREW

Skill level: Beginner

Time: 2 hours

Cost: Approx. $5

Driftwood
Basket

A DRIFTWOOD BASKET planted with colorful
flowers or a collection of decorative grasses and
heathers is the perfect accent for a lakeside cabin or
seaside cottage. If you can't find driftwood, build
your basket out of sturdy twigs and branches. If you
are lucky enough to be close to a beach that offers up
well-weathered driftwood on its shores, find the
most interesting pieces you can.

Materials

- Twelve pieces of driftwood, all approximately 1½' long (for the sides and bottom supports)
- Four pieces of 1½' driftwood, somewhat flatter, for the bottom
- One piece of curved driftwood, 1½' long, for the handle (optional)
- 2½" #8 screws
- A nail or scratch awl for making pilot holes

Tools

- Hammer
- Electric drill or screwdriver

Method

1. Collect all the driftwood to make the basket, laying it out in place to make sure the pieces fit together well. Bring it back to your work space.
2. Lay out the bottom pieces of the basket and lay the first two side pieces across the bottom slats. Attach the bottom support pieces by first making a small pilot hole with a hammer and nail or a scratch awl and then using the drill to attach the two pieces. (You can use a screwdriver to make the Driftwood Basket, but it will probably cost at least a few blisters. Driftwood is notoriously hard!)

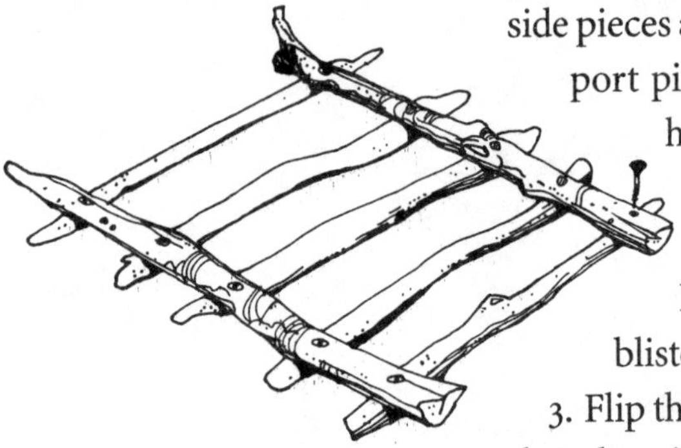

Figure 24-1

3. Flip the piece over and begin building the sides up on the other side, screwing each in place.
4. When you have reached the desired height, attach a curved piece for a handle if desired.

Decorative Grasses for Indoors and Outside

Indoor Grasses and Grass-like Plants

Acorus gramineus variegata

Arundinaria

Bambusa

Carex brunnea

Carex buchanani

Carex foiliosissima

Carex morrowii var. expallida

Carex phyllocephala

Cymbopogon citratus

Cyperus involucratus

Equisetum hyemale

Oplismenus

Sanservieria trifasciata

Scirpus cernuus

Setaria palmifolia

Stenotaphrum

Outdoor Grasses

Calamagrostis arundinacea

Helictotrichon sempervirens

Pennisetum alopecuroides

Setaceum

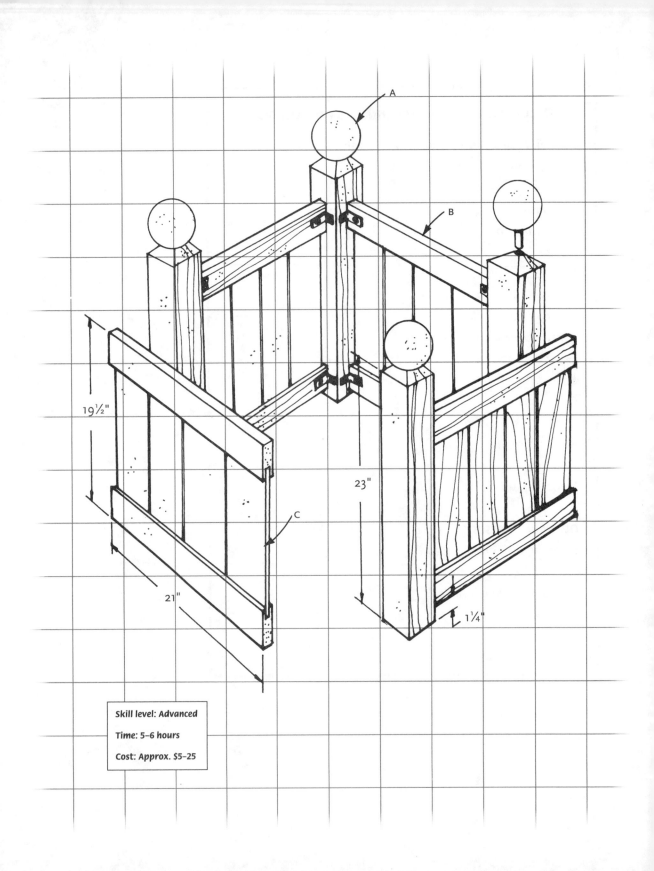

A

B

19½"

23"

C

21"

1¼"

Skill level: Advanced

Time: 5–6 hours

Cost: Approx. $5–25

Versailles Planter

V ERSAILLES PLANTERS are a very formal way to display small trees and shrubs. They originated in France and are traditionally painted white. Their most distinctive feature is the wooden ball on each of their four posts. A pair of Versailles planters on either side of a door makes an impressive entryway. Train a small tree into classical topiary form in each planter for a timeless and elegant look. This planter is made of cedar. Left unpainted, it will weather to a lovely gray outdoors.

Materials

- Four 23½" × 2½" × 2½" pieces of wood for the legs
- Eight 21" × 2¼" × 1¼" pieces of wood for the rails
- Twenty-four 17" × 3½" × ¾" pieces for the slats
- One 22¾" × 22¾" × ¾" piece of plywood for the bottom
- Sixteen 1" steel brackets (predrilled)
- Twelve 1½" steel brackets (predrilled)
- Six ½" screws
- Eight 1¼" screws
- Four hardwood balls 2½" in diameter
- Four dowels, 2" long and ½" in diameter

Tools

- Tablesaw and planer or jointer and handplane
- Square
- Ruler
- Tape measure
- Marking gauge
- Screwdrivers (Robertson or Phillips #1 and #2)
- Handsaw

Method

1. Cut the pieces of wood to the dimensions given.
2. Set the tablesaw to approximately 25° and cut each side of the leg tops until a point is created. You will need to use an auxiliary fence for this.
3. Rip a ¾" wide, 1" deep groove in one edge of each rail. The slats will fit into this groove.
4. Mark the insides of the legs 1¼" from the bottom. The bottom edges of the rails will align with these.
5. Attach the 1" brackets to the rails as shown on page 122. Do not center these on the face of the rail. Instead, put them 1" from the bottom edge on four rails, and 1" from the top edge on the other four rails.

6. Screw a rail between two legs. Align the ends of the brackets with the inside of the leg. Align the bottom of the rail with the 1¼" line.

7. Place six slats in the groove. Push the top rail onto these slats, making sure they are all still in the groove. Where the top rail bottoms out on the slats, screw it into place as was done with the bottom rail using eight 1¼" screws.

8. Repeat Steps 5 and 6 to make another side.

9. Lay one side face down on a workbench and attach the top and bottom rails to each leg (these should be standing straight up).

10. Slide slats into the grooves between the top and bottom rails. At this point you should have a three-sided, two-legged box.

11. Place the other finished side on top of the assembly and screw it into position from the inside.

12. Cut the plywood bottom to size. Using a handsaw, cut a 1" notch out of each corner.

13. Attach the 1½" brackets to the bottom, three per side, using six ½" screws.

14. With the planter on its side, insert the bottom. It should fit the brackets holding the rails to the legs. At this point, crawl in and screw the bottom to the rails using eight 1¼" screws.

15. To add the decorative wooden balls to the top of each leg, simply drill a ½" diameter hole 1¼" deep at the peak of the beveled end and another in the ball. Glue the dowel into the ball with carpenter's glue, then glue it into the top of the leg as shown in Figure 25-1.

16. Stain or paint the entire planter as desired.

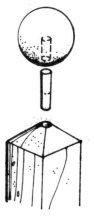

Figure 25-1

Training a Tree Standard

The painstaking process of training trees into topiary shapes has been giving Western gardeners pleasure for hundreds of years. The constant small efforts are richly rewarded when the vision you have in your head takes form in a tree. Both indoor and outdoor plants can be trained into classical topiary standards.

1. To begin, plant a single-stemmed seedling in a 6" pot and insert a length of bamboo approximately equal to the height of the finished tree.
2. Fasten the stem to the bamboo with a plastic twist-tie. Make sure you leave a bit of room for the stem to expand as it grows. Add another twist-tie every 4" or 5" as the tree grows.
3. Pinch or cut off new branches as the tree grows, leaving only the top growth. Let the leaves growing out of the stem remain and only remove them when the head of the tree begins to form.
4. When the stem reaches the desired height, pinch out the growing tip so that two branches will grow out of it. When these have a few sets of leaves, pinch out their growing tips. Repeat this until the head of the tree is the desired bushiness.
5. Make sure to repot the tree as necessary to provide room for the roots and to make sure the tree does not become top-heavy.

Popular Plants for Topiary Standards

Angel trumpet	Chinese hibiscus
Coleus	Flowering maple
Gardenia	Geraniums
Jasmine	Lantana
Rosemary	Sweet bay

Part 3

Containers and Covers

Containers and Covers

CONTAINERS AND COVERS provide the opportunity to hide an unprepossessing plastic pot inside a more attractive exterior. The possibilities are endless as interior designers have shown with their ingenious solutions for containers. Anything that will hold a potted plant is fair game.

Secondhand stores and flea markets are excellent sources for inexpensive containers. Brass pots make handsome containers and are widely available at flea markets at very low cost. Tin buckets and watering cans make charming containers indoors and out. You can also cover plain plastic pots with cloth or crocheted wire covers.

Converting odd objects into containers and placing them in your house or garden is the horticultural equivalent of a wink and a nudge. Object recycling to create containers is a great way to get into gardening with your kids. Odd covers and containers are also great for giving gifts of potted plants and flowers. Tired of the foil wrap around the potted mums? Make a cloth cover that can be used or recycled into a teapot cozy to hold your flower gift. Unusual containers and covers can also make witty table centerpieces or take-away gifts at place settings.

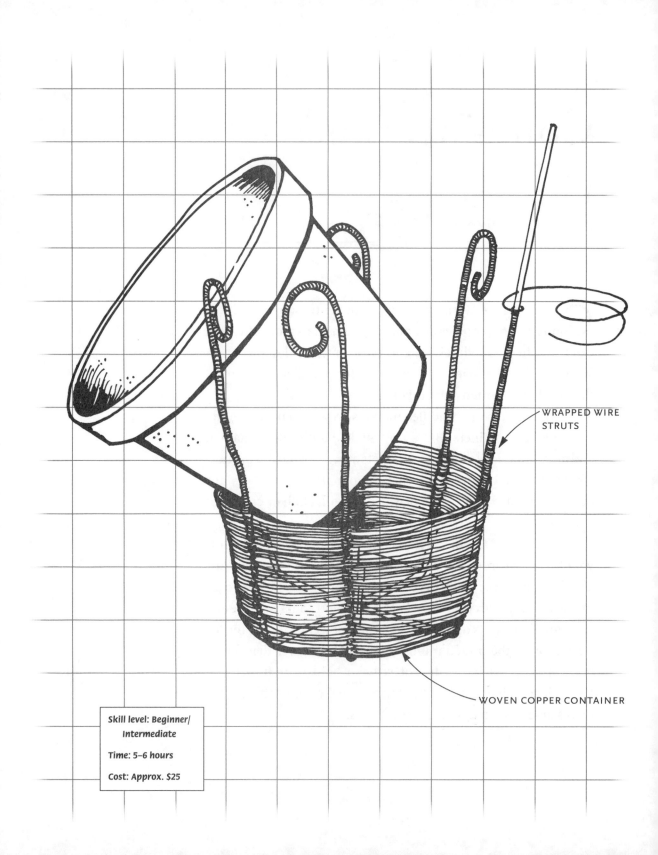

WRAPPED WIRE
STRUTS

WOVEN COPPER CONTAINER

Skill level: Beginner/
Intermediate

Time: 5–6 hours

Cost: Approx. $25

Wrapped and Woven Copper Wire Container

A VERY PRETTY setting for a favorite small plant, this project can be made into a hanger or used to accent a simple painted clay pot. The thin woven copper wire creates a delicate wire "fabric" which is set off with the saucy wrapped-copper curls around the top edges of the container.

Materials
- Fine-gauge copper wire (available at beading and some craft stores)
  Note: This very fine, almost thread-like copper wire is much easier to work than the heavier 20-gauge wire used in Project 5.
- 14-gauge wire
- Masking tape
- Acrylic paint

Tools
- Wire cutters
- Pliers
- Safety glasses

Method
1. To begin, cut three pieces of 14-gauge wire long enough to wrap around the outside of the pot (see Project 5). Bend each of your three pieces of wire around your upside-down pot, one at a time, so that they cup it from the bottom. There should be at least 3" of wire protruding above the top of the pot. Fold each of the top pieces down so that your pot fits securely in the wire cup.
2. Fasten the wire struts at the top of the pot with masking tape to hold them securely against the pot. You may need someone to hold the wires in place while you tape them.
3. Weave the fine copper wire around the struts.
4. When you near the top of the pot, unwrap the masking tape and bend out the wires tucked into the pot.
5. Wrap the wire struts with the copper wire, continuing to weave as you move from one to the next.
6. When all of the wire struts have been wrapped, use your pliers to make them into curls.

7. Paint the pot to complement the woven copper container and place it where people can admire the delicate copper "fabric" container you have created. These containers look particularly attractive planted with succulents.

A Note About Succulents

Succulents are any plants that are able to store water in their leaves or stems. The succulent group includes cactus, or the family Cactaceae.

Succulents (and cacti) are xerophytes, meaning that they can live with very little water. Their leaves and stems tend to be fleshy, to enable them to store water. Succulents are excellent choices for unusual containers because they are hardy and come in sizes from extremely tiny to very large. Succulents are also notable for their unusual forms. The most bizarre plants often fall into the succulent category.

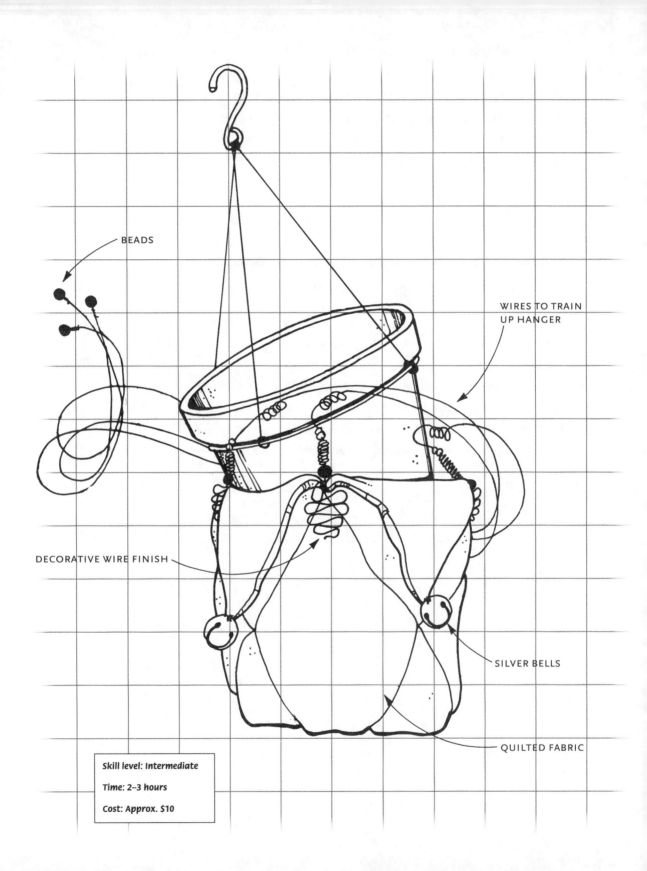

BEADS

WIRES TO TRAIN
UP HANGER

DECORATIVE WIRE FINISH

SILVER BELLS

QUILTED FABRIC

Skill level: Intermediate

Time: 2–3 hours

Cost: Approx. $10

Cloth Plant Bag

Design by Gail Hourigan

Plant bags are a stroke of genius by Vancouver craft designer Gail Hourigan. Ideal for covering the plain plastic pots with built-in wire hangers that are used to hang plants in a store, these are decorative enough to use with any pot. They make wonderful gift bags for plants as well. The "arms" of the plant bags are designed to cover the wire hanger "arms." Plant bags look great around potted flowers as well as hanging plants. I have been known to actually buy separate wire hanger arms to attach to pots so I have something to tie the attractive straps of the bag onto. Once your plant is in a plant bag you may not want to hang it (although the witty little bottom details make the hanging view particularly interesting).

Plant bags are easy to take on and off when you water your plant. If you don't want to be bothered with removing them, make the bags out of a waterproof fabric such as vinyl. This treatment will increase the humidity around your plant. Just be sure to wash out the bag every so often. Your fabric options are unlimited, but avoid fabrics that are easily spotted and stained by water. If you want to use waterproof fabrics, consider some of the fabrics used to make tablecloths.

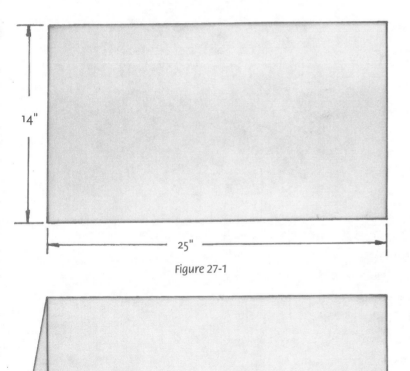

Figure 27-1

Figure 27-2

Materials

- Newspaper
- Approximately 1 square yard of fabric
- Thread
- ¼" quilt batting
- 10" of decorative cord
- Yarn
- Tassels
- Scraps of fabric
- Sewing glue
- Four small silver craft bells, available at sewing and craft stores (optional)
- Craft wire, available at beading and some craft stores (optional)
- Beads (optional)

Tools

- Sewing machine
- Crochet hook
- Scissors

Method

1. Cut the piece of newspaper so it is 14" × 25". Fold it in four, and then in half again (Figures 27-1 to 27-3).

2. Open the paper and take one of the patterns and pin it to the fabric, which should be folded in two, right sides together. Trace a point on the top of the paper and cut it out (Figure 27-4 to 27-5).

3. Remove the paper pattern and sew the fabric, right sides together, on one side and around the points, leaving the straight bottom edges of the bag open (Figure 27-6).

4. Turn the bag right side out and iron it.

5. Cut out one piece of quilt batting—the pattern less ¼" all the way around. Stuff the bag with the batting (Figure 27-7).

6. Sew diagonal triangles or any pattern or shape you desire over the stuffed bag (Figure 27-8).

7. Sew the two sides together to form the bag into a circle (Figure 27-9).

8. Turn the bag inside out, and sew the bottom seam closed to form the bottom of the bag (Figure 27-10).

9. Measure 3½" on each side from the center of the bottom seam. Sew a 5" dart at right angles to the bottom seam at each 3½" point. The dart will be approximately 2½" deep and will form the rounded bottom of the bag (Figure 27-11).

Figure 27-3

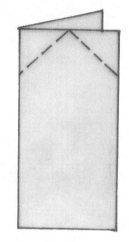

Figure 27-4

Figure 27-5

10. Turn the bag right side out and sew bells on each of the four points.

11. Cut the craft wire into three 4' lengths.

12. Bend the wire into a "squeezed" shape as shown (Figure 27-12).

13. Wrap the wire around the crochet hooks twelve times to make a spiral, right above the squeezed shape. Slip the wire off the hook.

14. Thread two or three beads onto the wires. Move 1" up each of the wires and thread a larger bead, feeding the wire back through the bead.

15. Add a bead or two on each of the ends of the wires.

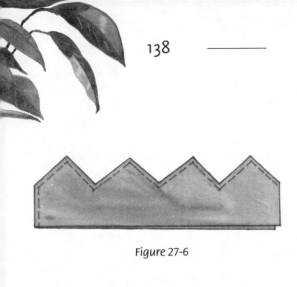

Figure 27-6

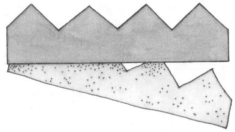

Figure 27-7

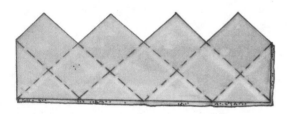

Figure 27-8

Figure 27-9

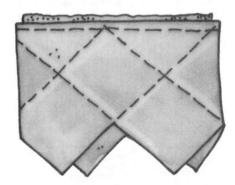

Figure 27-10

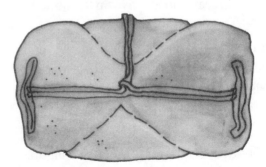

Figure 27-11

16. Sew the wire, between the squeezed shape and the spiral, between the points of the bag, on the outside.

Optional Trim (Cord and Tassels)

1. Cut the decorative cord into 5' lengths.
2. Wind the cord into a curl, pinning as you go until the cord curl is about 1" across. Glue or sew the cord circle together.
3. Cut a 1" diameter fabric circle and glue it to the glued side of the cord curl (Figure 27-13).
4. Glue the cord curls opposite one another, on either side of the cloth bag. You can also hand-sew the cord curls to the bag to attach them more securely.
5. Take the rest of the cord and tie it at the top so it fits over the wire hanger.
6. Sew tassels on each of the points.

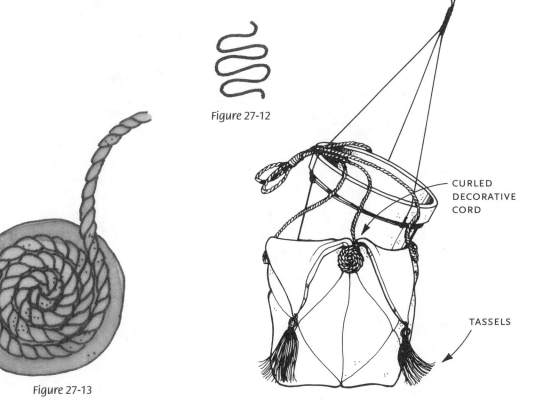

Figure 27-12

Figure 27-13

CURLED
DECORATIVE
CORD

TASSELS

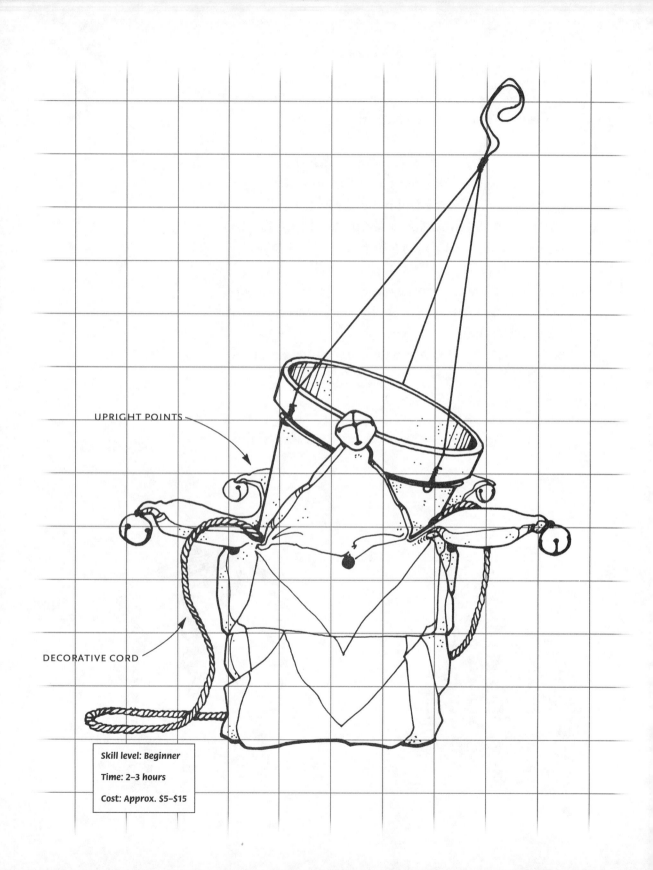

UPRIGHT POINTS

DECORATIVE CORD

Skill level: Beginner

Time: 2–3 hours

Cost: Approx. $5–$15

Crown Pointed Bag

Design by Gail Hourigan

T HIS PLANT BAG style is particularly suited to a more vertical type of plant. It wonderfully accents upright leaves.

Materials

- Newspaper
- ¼" quilt batting
- 1 square yard of fabric (try using pieces with contrasting textures for interest)
- Thread to match or contrast fabric
- Upholstery cord
- Four silver bells
- Tassel

Tools

- Sewing machine
- Scissors
- Crochet hook

Method

1. Use the pattern for the basic Cloth Plant Bag. Follow the directions until it comes time to stuff the quilt batting.
2. When stuffing the quilt batting, make sure to stuff the points of the bag very firmly, so they stand up.
3. Follow the directions as for the other project from this point on.
4. When it comes time to trim the bag, sew the bells on the upright points.
5. Sew a tassel on the middle of the bottom of the bag.
6. Cut a length of cord long enough to reach over the top of the hanger hook.
7. Sew the ends of the cords inside the bag.

Ribbon and Wire Trim

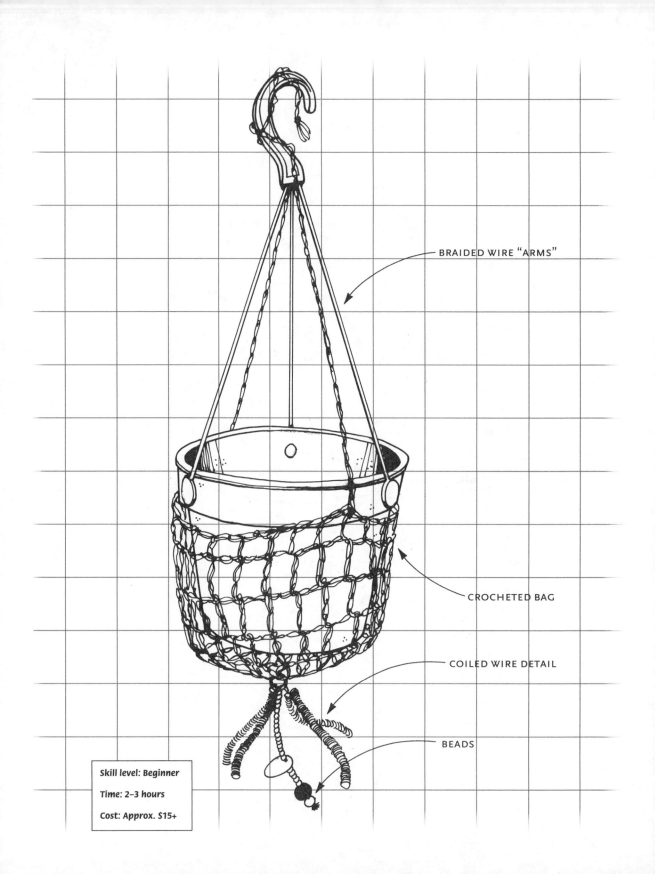

BRAIDED WIRE "ARMS"

CROCHETED BAG

COILED WIRE DETAIL

BEADS

Skill level: Beginner

Time: 2–3 hours

Cost: Approx. $15+

Crocheted Plant Bag

Design by Gail Hourigan

Crocheted plant bags are another invention by Gail Hourigan. They are designed to cover plain pots with built-in hangers. Crocheted wire bags have the added advantage that they don't have to be removed when you water your plants. I love the look of silvery blue-green wire with succulents, but any color wire will suit a variety of plants.

Materials
- Craft wire (available at beading and some craft stores)
- Beads

Tools
- 5.0 crochet hook
- Scissors

Method
1. Attach the wire with a slip knot to the crochet hook (Figure 29-1).
2. Work five chain stitches (Figures 29-2 to 29-4). Hook through the first stitch and join the two ends with a chain stitch to make a ring (Figures 29-5 and 29-6).

Slip Knot

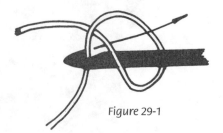

Figure 29-1

Chain Stitches

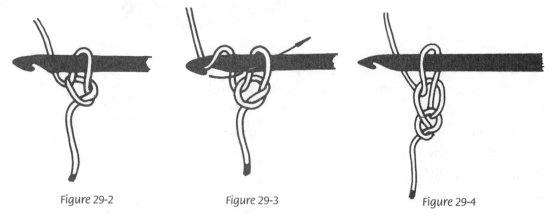

Figure 29-2   Figure 29-3   Figure 29-4

3. Second Row: Work two double half crochet stitches into each chain of the first row and join (Figures 29-7 to 29-10).

4. Third Row: Alternate two double half crochet, then three double half crochet stitches. Join.

5. Fourth Row: Work two double half crochet into each stitch for four stitches, then work three double crochet into one stitch (Figures 29-9 and 29-10). Repeat all the way around the row and join.

Chain Stitches into a Ring

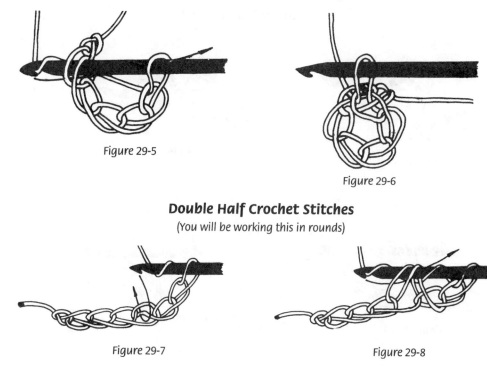

Figure 29-5

Figure 29-6

Double Half Crochet Stitches
(You will be working this in rounds)

Figure 29-7

Figure 29-8

Figure 29-9

Figure 29-10

6. Fifth Row: Work one double half crochet for three stitches, then work two double half crochet into one stitch. Repeat until the end of the row and join. These five rows will be the bottom of your plant bag.

7. Now work double crochet along each row, until you have reached the height of the pot you want your bag to cover (Figures 29-11 and 29-15).

Double Crochet Stitch
(You will be working this in rounds)

Figure 29-11

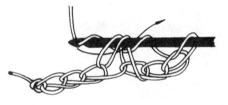

Figure 29-12

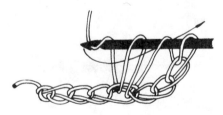

Figure 29-13

Figure 29-14

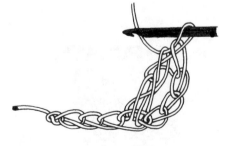

Figure 29-15

8. To make the ties, crochet single crochet lengths long enough to hold the crocheted bag on the plant hanger and attach them on opposite sides of the bag.
9. To make the tassel, wrap wire around the crochet hook until the coil is 3" long.
10. Add beads to the tops of the wire spiral coil.
11. Make several of these rolls, varying their tightness for contrast. Twist all of the coils together at one end. Attach them to the center bottom of the crocheted hanger.

Cacti and Succulents for a Crocheted Bag

Asparagus fern	*Asparagus densiflorus*
Century plant	*Agave americana marginata*
Partridge breast	*Aloe variegata*
Urn plant	*Aechmea fasciata*
Burro's tail	*Sedum morganianum*
Christmas cactus	*Schlumbergera*
	Hatiora bambusoides
	Hawthornia baccata
	Kalanchoe pinnata
	Kalanchoe manginii
Mistletoe cactus	*Rhipsalis cassutha*
Rat's tail	*Aporocactus flagelliformus*
Sun cactus	*Heliocereus speciosus*

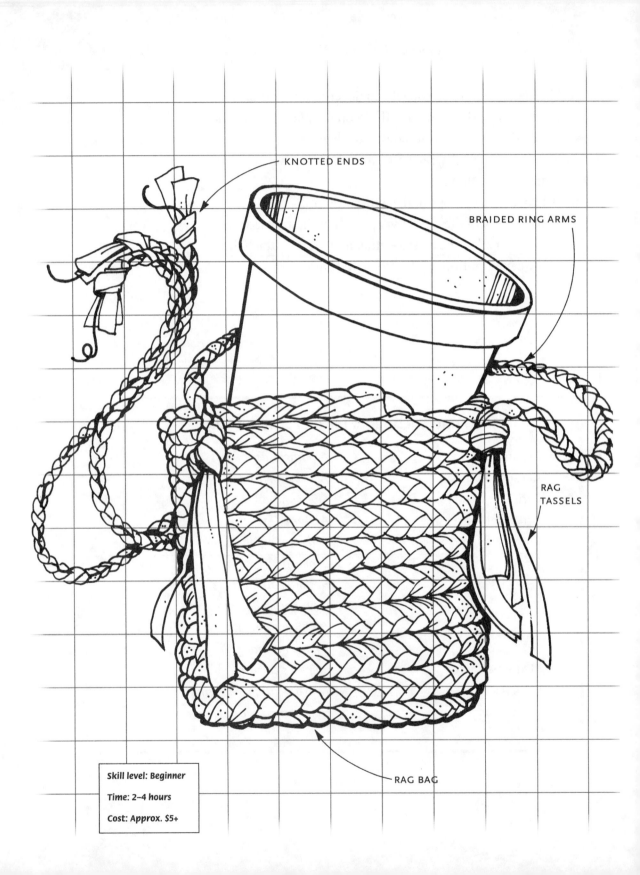

KNOTTED ENDS

BRAIDED RING ARMS

RAG
TASSELS

RAG BAG

Skill level: Beginner

Time: 2–4 hours

Cost: Approx. $5+

Rag Bag

Design by Gail Hourigan

T HE RAG BAG is a fabulous way to cover up a plain pot
with a built-in wire hanger. The braided bag makes a
richly textured setting for any plant. The bag can be designed
to complement your décor. For only pennies, the rag bag
will allow you to add interest to hanging plants. The coiled
braided arms set off spiky-leafed plants perfectly. The Rag
Bag is treated with a water-resistant spray to make sure it
doesn't get damaged. If your pot doesn't have a watering
saucer attached, then you can either fit one into the bag or
take the plant out to be watered.

Materials
- Strips of material that will not fray (such as synthetics) in different colors and textures. You may be able to use left-over fabric or go through the remnants bin at your local fabric shop. Old clothing is another good source for fabric.
- Tassel
- Several feet of 20-gauge wire
- Scotchgard™ or another spray-on water-resistant finish for fabric

Tools
- Scissors
- Thread
- Iron
- Sewing machine (optional)
- Sewing needle

Method
1. Cut lengths of fabric 1½" wide by 22½' long to make three separate strips with which to braid. The strips do not need to be perfectly straight. You may need to sew some of your strips together to make them long enough. You can sew together different materials in the same strip for interest.
2. Pull on the strips to make the raw side edges roll up (a tendency of most synthetic fabrics). You might have to iron or sew a strip into thirds if the wrong side keeps curling up.
3. Knot together your three strips of material, and secure them by hanging them on a nail or other object so you can work with them comfortably.
4. Roll up the excess length on each strip and secure it with a rubber band to make it convenient to braid with.
5. Braid up the entire length of strips.

6. Coil the braid in a circle to make the bottom of the rag basket. Pin the bottom coil together and sew it with an overcast stitch starting from the center. Do not sew too tightly or the stitches will pucker the braid (Figure 30-1).

7. To make the sides of the rag basket, coil the braid around the circle/bottom and pin in place. Make the rag cup big enough to extend just over the lip of the plant pot you want to cover.

8. Sew up the sides with overcast stitches. Turn the rag bag inside out so that the stitches are hidden.

9. Sew the tassel onto the bottom of the rag bag.

10. Cut six strips of fabric, each long enough to form two "arms" that can be wound up the wire arms of the hanger you are disguising.

11. Cut two pieces of 20-gauge wire, each long enough to braid into the fabric arms. Knot the tops and bottoms of the braided arms to secure them.

12. Sew the braided wire-stiffened arms to the bottom of the rag bag. Coil the arms tightly around your fingers or a pencil or some other round object to give them a spiral shape.

13. Spray the entire bag and its arms with a water-resistant spray-on finish. Allow it to dry.

14. Use the bag to cover a plain pot with a built-in hanger. Loosely wrap the coiled arms around the wire hanger rods and tie them at the top.

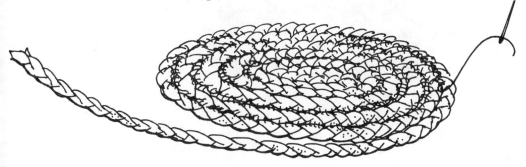

Figure 30-1

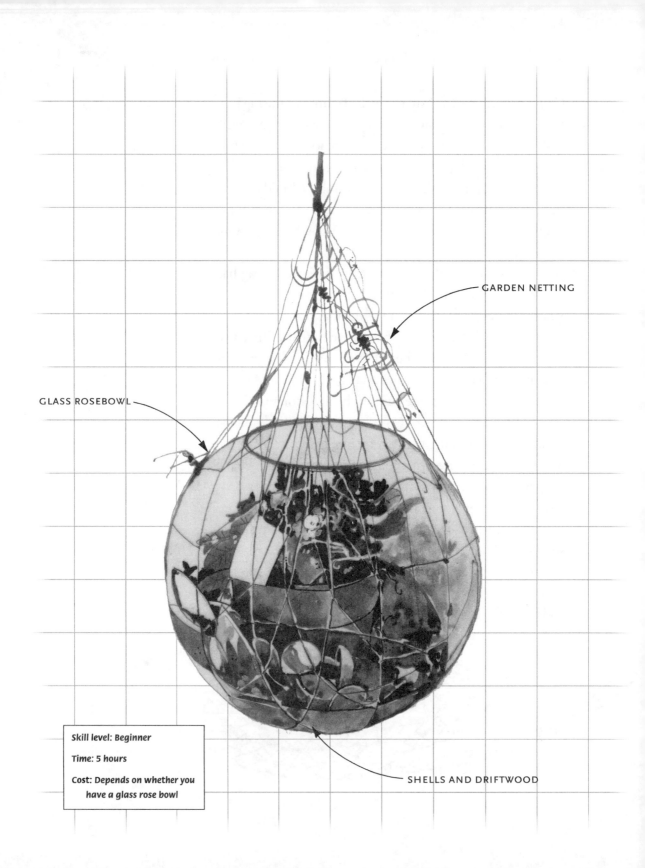

GARDEN NETTING

GLASS ROSEBOWL

Skill level: Beginner

Time: 5 hours

Cost: Depends on whether you
have a glass rose bowl

SHELLS AND DRIFTWOOD

Glass and Ceramic Containers

CONTAINERS ARE AMONG the simplest and most stylish ways to display potted plants. Cups, mugs, fish bowls, fish tanks, vases, and rose bowls are among a few of the glass containers that can beautifully accommodate plants. The substrate is what gives glass containers great visual impact and here again your options are almost endless.

Shown opposite is a rose bowl filled with a collection of shells and small pieces of driftwood with a flowering violet in a clay pot nestled among them. Hung with garden netting, the rose bowl would be a beautiful accent in a seaside cottage. Try using layers of sand in different colors in a large vase and add a small pot filled with decorative grasses to complete the impression of lakeside charm.

For a romantic effect, fill a glass container with small rocks in various colors. Cover the bottom of the container with water and then place "Paperwhites" or hyacinth bulbs on top. The bulbs' roots will reach down through the pebbles to the water below. The bulbs will sprout and eventually bloom to complete the display. Use moss, twigs, and pinecones to disguise pots nestled in a large clear glass container for a woodsy effect.

Marbles, coins, beads, and buttons are just a few more materials that can surround a potted plant in a glass.

Finally, if you are a fan of all things small, plant a pair of dainty matching teacups with baby's breath. The effect is delightful, particularly if it is accompanied by a planted antique teapot.

Country Charm

Consider hanging simple garden flowers in glass jars for a charming effect. Vases and drinking glasses with lips can also be suspended in this manner. Use rope, ribbon, or raffia to hang the cut flowers from a nail or hook.

Pretty rustic flower arrangements:

Baby's breath	Black Eyed Susan
Daisies	Grasses
Everlasting	Bachelor's Buttons
Poppies	Carrot fronds
Purple coneflowers	Sweetpeas

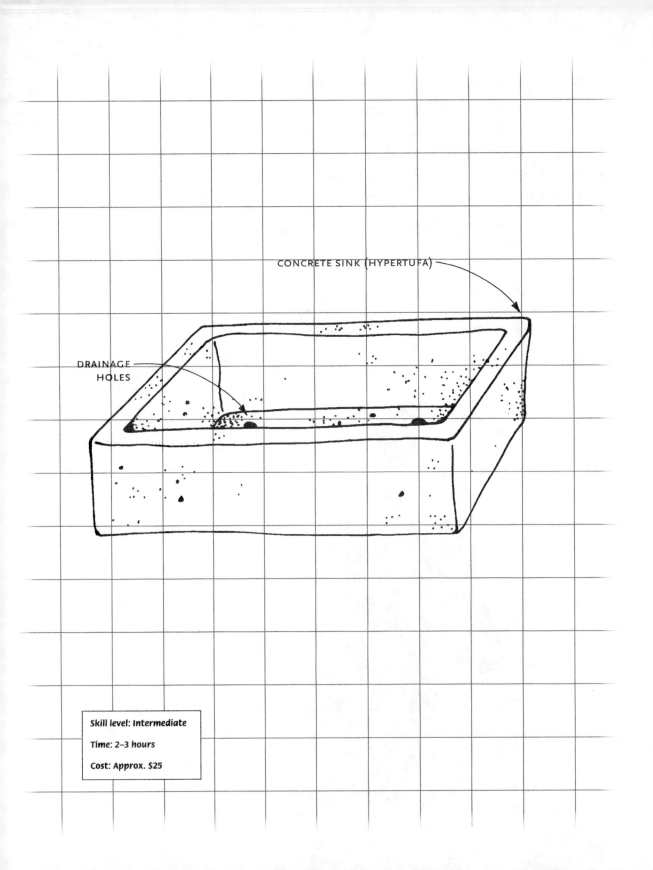

CONCRETE SINK (HYPERTUFA)

DRAINAGE HOLES

Skill level: Intermediate

Time: 2–3 hours

Cost: Approx. $25

Concrete Alpine Planter (Hypertufa)

ALSO KNOWN as hypertufa, concrete containers designed to house alpine plants have a surprisingly organic appearance, given their constructed nature. The rough and weathered gray of the concrete perfectly suits the delicate coloring and silvery cast of tiny alpine plants. Concrete containers are not difficult to make, but they do take a long time to dry and cure. Your hypertufa will not be ready to use for at least two months. The Alpine Planter needs time to cure and should be left outside for rainwater or frequent rinsings with a hose to leach the lime out of the concrete.

Materials
- Concrete mix
- Sand
- Two cardboard boxes that fit inside each other with a 1"–2" gap between them (they can be cut to fit)
- Chicken wire or wire mesh
- Four pieces of ½" doweling, 6" long
- Heavy tape

Tools
- Razor blade or kitchen knife
- Rubber gloves
- Wire cutters
- Scraper
- Bucket
- Protective sheeting (for the floor)
- Spray bottle for water

Method
Find a place to work where you can make a mess. Protect the area with plastic sheeting.

1. Fit the boxes inside one another. If necessary, cut the smaller one to fit and tape it securely. If you want to get creative you can use round forms or other shapes to make suitable molds. The outer box should be at least 10" deep and the smaller one should be 3"–4" shallower. The smaller box will be placed upside down into the outer box after the concrete has been poured, so test the fit with the smaller box flipped over (Figure 32-1). Reinforce the outer box with tape so it is able to withstand the weight of the concrete (Figure 32-2).

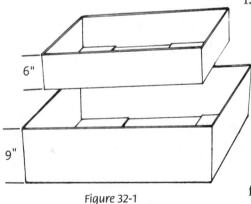

6"

9"

Figure 32-1

2. Mix one part concrete and three parts sand.

3. Pour approximately 1" of the concrete mixture into the bottom of the large box and then cut a piece of chicken wire to fit the bottom of the box.

4. Place the dowels upright into the mixture and through the wire so they create drainage holes, and then pour another inch of concrete into the bottom of the box (Figure 32-3).

5. Now fit the smaller box upside down into the middle of the larger box. Wrap the smaller box with a piece of chicken wire that reaches all the way around and to the top. Press the small box and wire into the layer of concrete at the bottom of the box.

6. Fill the gap between the boxes with concrete so that the wire around the small box is completely covered (Figure 32-4). Add the mix a small amount at a time. Let the whole box sit for three days at room temperature.

7. After three days, take off the outside box and lightly spray the concrete box with water. Let it sit for another week.

8. After a week or so, take out the inner box and doweling and let the box sit for several days. (You might find your project makes you unpopular with the rest of the family if it is left in their way for days on end while it cures. The extensive curing time is one very good reason not to construct and leave your hypertufa on the dining room table!)

9. Now take the concrete container and let it sit outside for at least a month. Let rainwater leach the lime from the concrete or, if you live

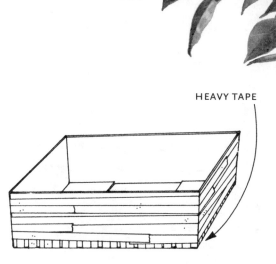

HEAVY TAPE

Figure 32-2

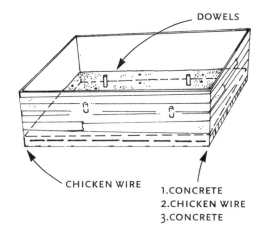

DOWELS

CHICKEN WIRE

1. CONCRETE
2. CHICKEN WIRE
3. CONCRETE

Figure 32-3

in a dry climate, water the trough every few days and let the water drain away until all the lime has been removed. If you plant the concrete container before the lime is gone it will kill the plants.

Note: For a round hypertufa, follow these same basic instructions, but use two very large plastic bowls that fit inside one another.

Figure 32-4

Planting a Hypertufa

Hypertufa are most often used for alpines but can also serve as housing for any tiny plants. To plant an alpine garden in your concrete rock garden, you will need a liner for the bottom of the container, alpine potting mixture, decorative rocks, and a selection of small alpine plants. Or you can mix tiny trees and shrubs with bulbs and perennials for a lovely display. Also try succulents.

Alternative Method

The following is an alternative method of building a hypertufa. It should be done outside and under a covering or in a shed. This method will work well if you are having trouble finding two cardboard boxes or two plastic bowls that fit inside one another.

1. Form a rectangle of moist sand on a plastic sheet. The sand should be about 1" thick and just a bit longer and wider than the finished hypertufa will be. Place a series of bricks on the bed of sand to create the form for the hypertufa.

2. Cover the bricks with a piece of plastic sheeting, tucked in neatly around and under the bricks.

3. Shape the sand extending around the bricks so that it forms a channel for the rim.

4. Mix three parts sand to one part cement and, using a trowel, spread the mixture up the sides and over the top of the bricks. You must build up from the sides because the concrete won't stick to the plastic sheeting. Make sure the concrete mix is at least ½" thick around the bricks.

5. Wrap the concrete in chicken wire to reinforce the shape. Fold the wire at the corners so it wraps around neatly.

6. Place four pieces of doweling through the concrete and wire so that they touch the bricks. These will be the drainage holes.

7. Add another layer of the concrete mixture so that the depth of the concrete is approximately 2" in total (Figure 32-7).

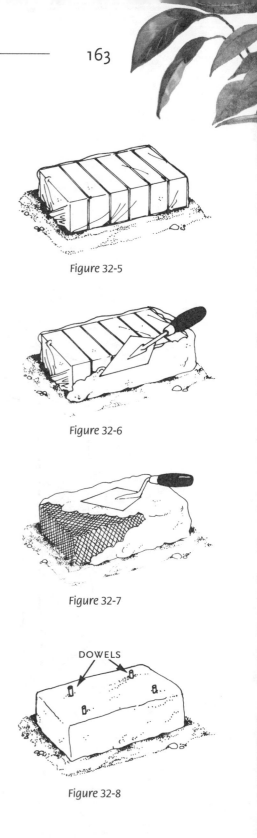

Figure 32-5

Figure 32-6

Figure 32-7

DOWELS

Figure 32-8

8. After the concrete has had time to set (approximately four days), lift the hypertufa from the bricks. It should slide off easily.

9. Remove the plastic sheeting and take out the dowels, making sure the drainage holes are open.

10. Use a hose to rinse off the hypertufa. Repeat the rinsing every few days for at least a month and a half, or leave it out in the rain for two months until it is ready to use.

Figure 32-9

A Selection of Alpine and Miniature Plants

Alyssum saxatile

Alyssum spinosum

Arabis caucasica

Aubrieta deltoidea

Cassiope lycopodiodes

Chamaecyparis obtusa

Corokia cotoneaster

Cryptomeria japonica

Dionysia tapetodes

Erinus alpinus

Helianthemum nummularium

Iberis sempervirens

Juniperus communis

Juniperus sabina

Juniperus squamata

Narcissus traiandus albus

Phlox douglasii

Phlox subulata

Picea glauca

Raoulia australis

Raoulia lutescens

Rosa chinensis

Salix repens

Saponaria ocymoides

Saxifraga burseriana

Sedum acre

Sedum spathulifolium

Sempervivum montanum

Thuja orientalis

Thymus serpyllum

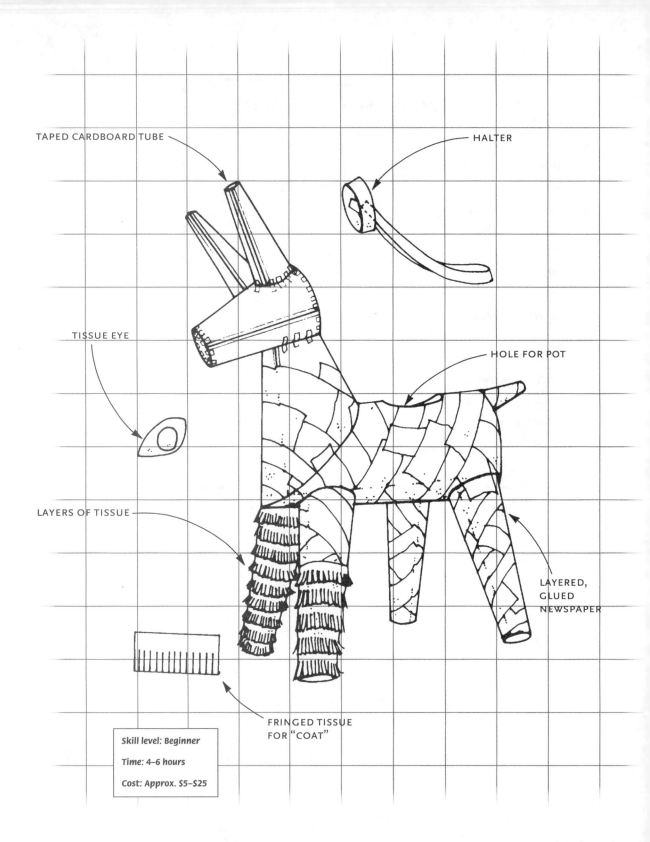

TAPED CARDBOARD TUBE

HALTER

TISSUE EYE

HOLE FOR POT

LAYERS OF TISSUE

LAYERED,
GLUED
NEWSPAPER

FRINGED TISSUE
FOR "COAT"

Skill level: Beginner

Time: 4–6 hours

Cost: Approx. $5–$25

Piñata Planter

THE PIÑATA PLANTER is the perfect project to do with kids. They will enjoy making the donkey, and be fascinated by the plants that fit into it. The Piñata Planter is also a fun way to present a gift of cacti to someone who collects them. You can use this technique to create plant holders in almost any shape you can think of. The plants you use should, however, be plants that require little water or spraying, because even when it has been treated with polyurethane spray, you still won't want to get your planter too wet.

Materials
- Several pieces of heavy cardboard (a pair of packing boxes will work well)
- Tape
- Newspaper
- White glue
- Selection of tissue paper in bright colors
- Short length of rope
- One small clay pot (approximately 4"-6" in diameter
- Two small half-baskets (to be used as saddle bags)
- 20-gauge wire
- Spray adhesive
- Polyurethane spray

Tools
- Small handsaw
- Scissors
- Face mask (for spraying the varnish)

Method

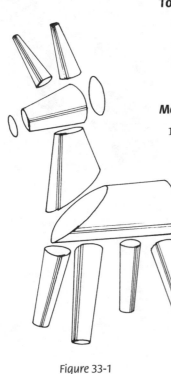

1. Cut the cardboard into pieces and fashion tubes to represent the donkey's body, four legs, neck, and head. These tubes can be joined using tape.

2. Once you have made all the cardboard body parts, tape them together to form the donkey.

3. Cut the newspaper into long, 1" wide strips, and in a bowl combine a mixture of half water to half glue.

4. Wet the strips, one at a time, and smooth them over the cardboard body of the donkey.

Figure 33-1

Cover the whole donkey with a single layer of wet newspaper and let it dry.

5. Cover the donkey with another layer of wet newspaper and glue and let dry.

6. Cut the tissue paper into strips, approximately 2" × 4". Cut the ends of the strips to make a fringe (cut several at once to save time).

7. Spray the donkey body with spray adhesive and attach the uncut ends of the colored tissues to the body, leaving the fringe end loose. Start at the bottom of the donkey and work up, layering the tissue onto the body.

8. Cut out several strips of tissue to make a bridle and glue it onto the donkey's nose.

9. Cut out two eyes and glue them onto the donkey's head.

10. When the donkey is dry, spray it several times with polyurethane spray, letting it dry between coats.

11. Cut a hole in the donkey's back that will accommodate a small pot. Plant the pot with a cactus or several cacti and fit the pot into the donkey's back.

12. Tie a length of rope between the two half-baskets and place them over the donkey's back like saddle bags. Fill them with small cacti.

13. If you like, you can attach a length of wire through the donkey's shoulders to allow you to suspend or carry it. If you choose to hang your piñata, take care not to overload it.

Skill level: Beginner

Time: 1 hour

Cost: Approx. $2

Old Boots and Other Oddball Containers

Not necessarily tasteful or elegant, oddball containers have the equally important quality of being fun! The key to the successful oddball container is recycling. The main criteria for an oddball container are: Can you fit a plant in it? Will you get a kick out of it? And can you throw it away without regret when you are tired of it? Then use it! These old boots are just one example of the kinds of items that can be turned into plant containers. Use them to line the porch steps to your country cabin or the path to the tool shed. And don't stop with old boots. Olive oil tins, mason jars, lunch buckets, old mugs, coffee containers and many more objects will perform admirably as plant containers, for a season or even a few short weeks. You can just place your potted plants inside your object, or customize it so you can plant directly inside it.

Materials

- Spray paint
- Acrylic paints (optional)
- Polyurethane spray
- An old pair of boots (workboots or rubber boots are ideal)
- Burlap
- Small rocks or lava rocks
- Soil

Tools

- Face mask

Method

1. Spray paint the boots outside, using a mask. Let them dry.
2. Paint the boots with any designs you like using acrylic paints. Let dry.
3. Spray the boots with a polyurethane spray.
4. Cut two pieces of burlap, large enough to line the insides of the boots.
5. Place the potted plants directly inside the boots, or fill the boots with a layer of lava rocks for drainage and then a layer of soil. Then remove the plants from their pots, and place them inside the boots, filling in any gaps with extra soil.

Possible Oddball Containers

Tins of all types—vintage are best.

(Consider planting a collection of olive oil tins with Italian herbs such as basil, oregano, and sage. For another fitting combination, plant a coffee tin with a dwarf coffee bush, Coffee arabica 'Nana.')

Dishes, including bowls and mugs

Hollowed-out logs and pieces of wood

Old street light covers

Old bathroom fixtures, such as sinks

Chair missing a seat

(To plant, place a piece of chicken wire in the seat hole so it hangs down, line the seat with moss, fill with soil, and plant. Place so it doesn't tempt the weary to sit on the flowerbed seat.)

Old hammock

(Hang between two trees, line with moss, and plant.)

Old doll houses

Old chests

Wheelbarrows

Holes in bricks

Old birdhouses

Suitable plants

Fill boots with carnations, mums, pansies, daisies, or other hardy, unpretentious flowering plants.

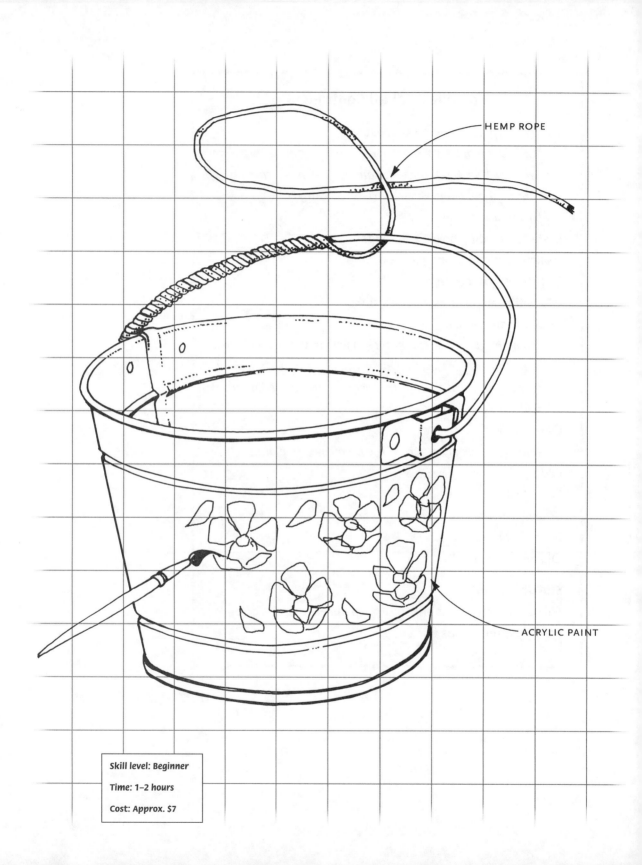

HEMP ROPE

ACRYLIC PAINT

Skill level: Beginner

Time: 1–2 hours

Cost: Approx. $7

Project 35

Painted
Tin Pail
Container

Folksy and inexpensive, a tin pail can be made into something special with paint and a bit of rope. The paint technique used on this pail is a version of a technique popular with folk artists throughout the world. It involves painting simplified brushstroke flowers and foliage. Tin pails make ideal containers for plants. They cost little, and come in many shapes and sizes. Tin pails have a rustic charm that is perfect for a kitchen.

Materials

- Tin pail
- Thin natural rope
- Painter's tape
- Chalk
- Selection of acrylic paints
- Clear polyurethane spray

Tools

- Scissors
- Several small paintbrushes, both flat and round

Method

1. Wrap painter's tape around the top and bottom thirds of the tin. Paint the area inside the tape with a coat of acrylic paint. Let the paint dry.
2. Following the directions for Painting Folk Art Flowers on page 177, outline the shapes of the flowers in chalk and then paint them in. Add centers to the flowers using a smaller brush and a different color. Add green foliage under and around the flowers.
3. When the paint is dry, spray the entire tin with a coat of polyurethane spray.
4. When the clear coat is dry, wrap the handle of the pail with rope.
5. I recommend leaving your plant inside its pot and using the pail as a container rather than a planter.

The Painted Tin Pail container looks wonderful holding a pot of sunny daisies, or other round and "simple" flowers.

Painting Folk Art Flowers

The naïve, bold appearance of folk art flowers depends on a set of traditional and very simple brush strokes. Daisies like the ones painted on this pot can be first outlined in chalk, then painted in as shown.

For full front daisies, draw a very light circle and divide it in four. Paint in petals as shown using a small round brush. Dab in the center of the flower using the end of your brush or another small round object.

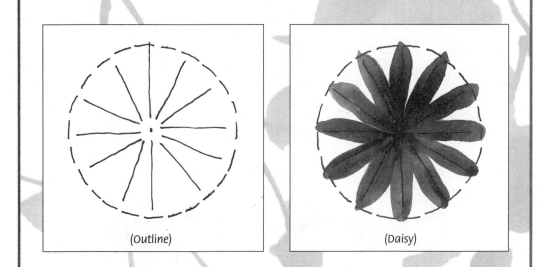

(Outline)   (Daisy)

To show the daisies at an angle, draw in a light oval and paint the petals into that, so that the petals at the back and front are foreshortened.

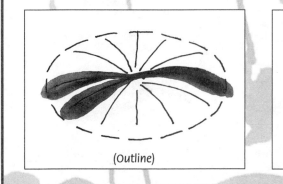

(Outline)

(Daisy on Angle)

Painting Folk Art Flowers continued

Other popular folk art strokes used to create folk art florals are the basic comma stroke done with a round or a flat brush, the crescent stroke with a round or flat brush, and the "S" stroke with a round or flat brush.

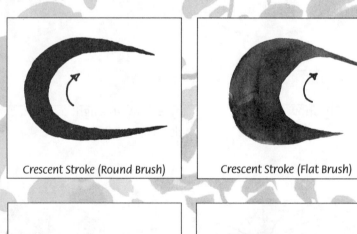

Basic Comma Stroke (Round Brush)

Basic Comma Stroke (Flat Brush)

Crescent Stroke (Round Brush)

Crescent Stroke (Flat Brush)

"S" Stroke (Round Brush)

"S" Stroke (Flat Brush)

Painting Folk Art Flowers continued

The scroll stroke (flat brush) and the circle stroke (flat brush) are combined to create wonderful floral designs, such as the traditional chrysanthemum shown below.

Scroll Stroke (Flat Brush)

Circle Stroke (Flat Stroke)

Traditional Folk Flower

Part Four

Sconces, Stands, and Tables

Sconces, Stands, and Tables

B Y ELEVATING your plants on tables or stands, they will take on the aspect of natural objets d'art. The same principle applies to sconces. It is one thing to add a plant to the side of a table crowded with knickknacks—and quite another to give a plant center stage. The effect of a plant displayed on a stand or plant table is striking. And if you choose the right plant for this honor, it will have as big a design impact in your room as a piece of art.

The sconces, tables, and stands in this section vary from fine woodworking projects to simple assemblies with inexpensive materials. If you are planning a permanent display and enjoy woodworking, tackle the Japanese Plant Tables. Elegant and understated, they make the perfect display places for a pair of orchids or bonsai or any other plants that deserve the spotlight. If you have just purchased a large showy plant whose blooms will last only a few weeks, consider making a Bamboo and Raffia Stand to hold it during the plant's glory days. I did this recently with an orchid cactus in full bloom. For the duration of its flowering period it lived in a focal part of the living room where it drew oohs and aahs from admiring guests. Now it has retired to the bedroom, where its less spectacular aspect enhances a corner shelf. The Bamboo and Raffia Stand can also be appropriate as a permanent home for a tropical plant.

Sconces are yet another excellent space-saving way to display plants. Both interior and exterior locations will suit the simple and attractive Chicken Wire Sconces on page 187. Keep plants on permanent display in your sconces, or hang them to show off flowering plants.

Don't be afraid to treat some varieties of potted indoor plants as you would cut flowers. When they are spent, discard them. Reflect the seasons in your indoor potted plant displays. And make full use of potted tables and stands and sconces by changing the plants you keep on and in them. Many short-lived or at least short-blooming indoor plants are the same price as or less than cut flowers. Take full advantage of the ever-changing beauty they can provide inside the home.

Finally, sconces, stands, and tables allow you to maximize the visual effect of lushness by staggering the heights of your plants. By varying the levels you can address your plants' different light requirements and create interest for the onlooker. Far more appealing than a neat row of potted plants the same size is a collection of plants filling up a space. A large floor plant flanked by a slender plant stand and a sconce spilling ivy will create excitement in even the most mundane corner.

Plants with Presence

Amaryllis   *Hippeastrum evansiae*
Impatiens (for constant flowering display)
Begonias of all types (for flowering display)
Ivy Tree   *Fatshedera lizei*
Jade plant   *Crassula argentea*
                                                                  Hoffmanrefulgens
                                                                  (for a dark striking
                                                                  plant with a sculptural shape)

Rosemary, geranium, ivy, ficus
varieties, and pelargonium trained
into small topiary forms or espaliered
look great displayed by themselves
 on a table or stand.

                                                                  Nidularium hybrid

Ornamental pepper plants
Forsythia
Button fern   *Pellaea rotundi folia*
                                                                  Kalanchoe porphyrocalyx
                                                                  Guzmania lingulata

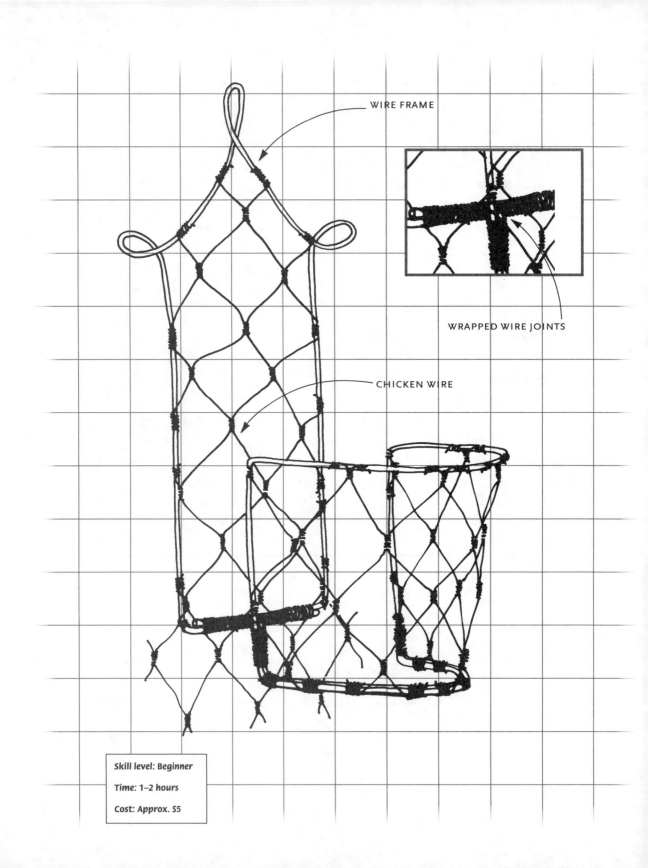

WIRE FRAME

WRAPPED WIRE JOINTS

CHICKEN WIRE

Skill level: Beginner

Time: 1–2 hours

Cost: Approx. $5

Project 36

Chicken Wire Sconce

T HIS CHICKEN WIRE sconce transcends its
humble materials and brightens any wall. Easy
to make, it will look wonderful inside or outside
and the glint of wire against a painted pot is striking. Use it to hang potted flowers or a trailing plant.
A chicken wire sconce fits into almost any décor
and will save table and shelf space.

187

Materials

- Approximately 5' of 14-gauge wire
- Approximately 15' of 20-gauge galvanized wire (preferably in black to contrast the frame and chicken wire)
- A large piece of chicken wire (approx. 2' × 4') with wide holes
- A 10" pot (You should have your pot handy to measure from while you make your sconce cup frames.)
- Clear tape

Tools

- Wire cutters
- Pliers
- Safety glasses

Method

1. To make the frame, cut a 3' piece of 14-gauge wire and bend it into the shape shown (Figure 36-1) with your pliers.
2. Tape the bottom of the frame and then wrap it with wire along the length of the bottom (Figure 36-1).
3. Bend the rest of the 12-gauge wire into a half-circle cup to hold the pot, measuring it against the size of your pot. Remember that your pot is smaller at the bottom than the top and when it is hanging, it should angle outward (Figure 36-2). Fasten the cup frame to the back frame with tape and 20-gauge wire.

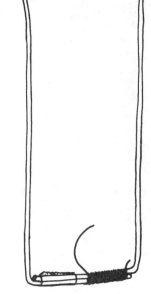

Figure 36-1

Figure 36-2

4. Lay the sconce against the piece of chicken wire and cut around it (Figure 36-3), leaving approximately 1" of wire ends to wrap the chicken wire onto the frame. Using your pliers, make sure all of the sharp ends of the chicken wire are tucked securely around the frames.

5. Cut two pieces of chicken wire to fit the bottom of the sconce and wrap them to the cup, using the loose wire ends. By doubling the wire at the bottom of the sconce you will increase its strength.

6. Cut a piece of chicken wire to fit around the outside of the cup and fasten it with the wire ends.

7. Hang the sconce with nails, using the loops at the top and sides.

Note: This project can be modified to fit different pots. Also, you can measure the bottom of your sconce to fit a saucer for your pot. Just remember that the saucer will be sitting on a bit of an angle and so if overfilled, may spill down the wall.

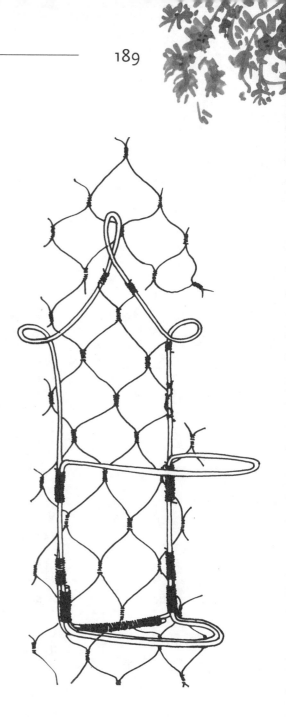

Figure 36-3

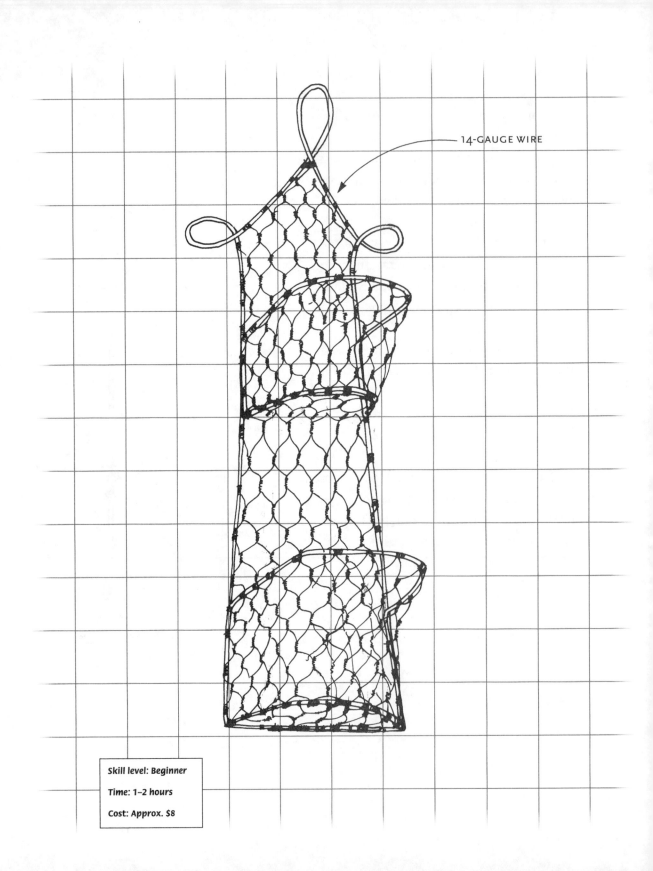

14-GAUGE WIRE

Skill level: Beginner

Time: 1–2 hours

Cost: Approx. $8

Chicken Wire Sconce for Two Pots

DOUBLE THE RUSTIC charm with a two-pot chicken wire sconce. Create several of these double sconces to hold your seedlings in the greenhouse (making sure to provide adequate drainage) or keep them inside to hold dwarf varieties of your favorite plants. Like the single chicken wire sconce, the double sconce can be adapted to fit different-sized pots. Just remember that the frame has to be strong enough to hold two pots, and the proportions of this design seem to work best with smaller (4"–6") pots.

Materials

- 14-gauge wire
- 20-gauge galvanized wire (preferably in black to contrast the frame and chicken wire)
- A large piece of chicken wire (approximately 2' × 6') with standard holes
- Two 4"–6" pots (You should have your pots handy to measure from while you make your sconce cup frames.)
- Clear tape

Tools

- Wire cutters
- Pliers
- Safety glasses

Method

1. To make the double-sconce frame, cut a 4' piece of 14-gauge wire and bend it into shape with your pliers.
2. Tape the bottom of the frame and then wrap it with wire along the length of the bottom.
3. Take the remaining 2' of wire and cut it in half. Form each piece into two half-circle cups to hold your pots, measuring the two cups against your pots. Remember that your pots are smaller at the bottom than the top and when they are hanging, they should angle outward. Fasten the cup frames to the back frame with tape and wire.
4. Lay the sconce against the piece of chicken wire and cut around it, leaving approximately 1" of wire ends to wrap the chicken wire onto the frame.
5. Cut four pieces of chicken wire to fit the bottoms of the two cups and wrap them onto the cups, using the loose wire ends. By doubling the chicken wire you increase the strength of the cups

6. Cut two pieces of chicken wire to fit around the cups and fasten them with the wire ends.

7. Hang the sconces with nails, using the loops at the top and sides.

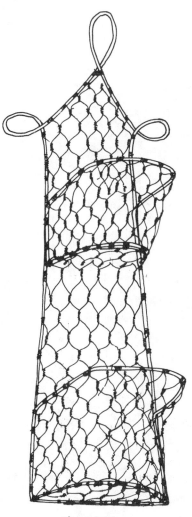

Figure 37-1

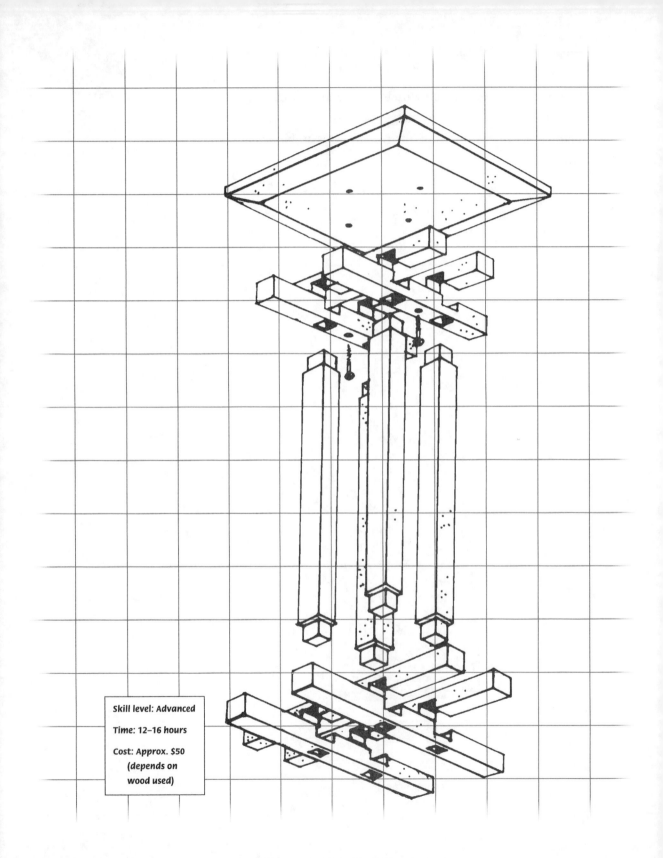

Skill level: Advanced

Time: 12–16 hours

Cost: Approx. $50
(depends on
wood used)

Project 38

Japanese Plant Tables

F OR A DISPLAY of formal elegance, consider a pair of Japanese-style plant tables. Built using traditional Japanese woodworking techniques and designed to reflect the spare grace and beauty found in all Japanese woodworking, these tables, holding a few special plants, will strike an elegant note wherever they are placed. This project is for the advanced woodworker and will require a good knowledge of handling tools and basic woodworking procedure. If you love these tables but aren't up to building them, consider taking the plans to your local cabinetmaker or an avid hobbyist and having them built for you. These pieces will last more than a lifetime and you are sure to treasure the opportunity they give you to combine two arts: gardening and woodworking.

Design by Aaron Banta

Materials

Top

• 10½" × 10½" × ¾" piece of wood

Legs

• Four ¾" × ¾" × 22½" pieces of wood (short table)

• Four ¾" × ¾" × 37¼" pieces of wood (tall table)

Top Assembly

• Four 7¼" × ¾" × ¾" pieces of wood

Bottom

• Four 13½" × ¾" × ¾" pieces of wood

• 6 1¼" screws

Tools

• Ruler

• Square

• Tablesaw

• Chisel

• #100 and #220 grit sandpaper

• Screwdriver

• White glue

• Wax or oil to finish.

Note: Top and bottom assemblies are built the same way; using a through mortise half lap joint.

Method

1. The method for making the top and bottom assemblies is exactly the same. The only difference is in the length of the four legs. With the legs cut to the length you prefer, cut a tenon ½" square × ¾" long at each end of each leg.

2. Cut the pieces for the top and bottom assemblies to length and mark the center point of each. The center of each leg is 1⅞" to either side of this center line.

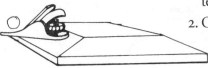

Figure 38-1

3. With a pencil and square, mark out the exact location of each leg, each mortise, and each half lap joint.

4. With a drill and chisel, cut out each ½" square mortise.

5. Sand all the pieces until the parts are smooth to touch.

6. Glue each assembly, making sure each one is square.

7. Screw on the top from underneath, making sure the screws are not too long.

8. Wax or oil to finish, following the manufacturer's instructions.

Making a Lap Joint

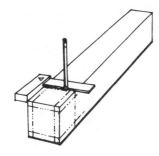

Figure 38-2

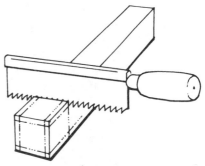

Figure 38-3

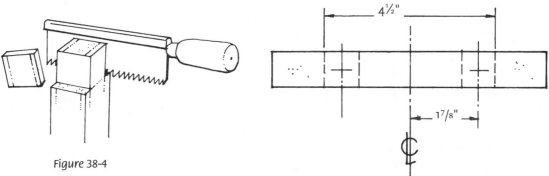

Figure 38-4

Figure 38-5

Making a Lap Joint continued

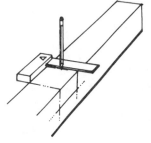

Figure 38-6

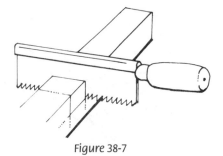

Figure 38-7

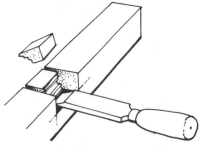

Figure 38-8

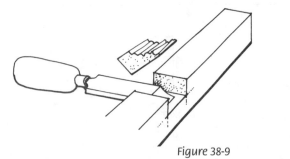

Figure 38-9

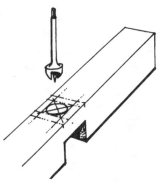

Figure 38-10

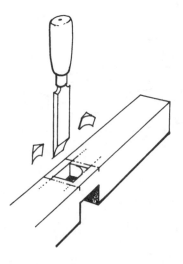

Figure 38-11

Figure 38-12

Bonsai

The plants we know as bonsai (bone-sigh) originated hundreds of years ago in Japan. They existed even before that in China, where they were known as *penjing*.

Bonsai is a demanding horticultural pursuit: it is the art and science of keeping a tree or shrub in a very small tray. Bonsai are kept small by pruning and pinching off their roots and branches when they are planted, and their branches as the plants grow. Bonsai are repotted frequently to help them maintain their size and shape.

Traditional bonsai are outdoor plants, and they are generally kept outside in the summer and overwintered in a cold greenhouse. Bonsai can also be grown using tropical plants and kept indoors year-round. Some typical indoor bonsai are:

Banyan tree	*Ficus retusa nitida*
Box honeysuckle	*Lonicera nitida*
Dwarf black olive	*Bucida spinosa*
False heather	*Cuphea hyssopifolia*
Japanese privet	*Ligustrum japonicum*
Powder puff	*Calliandra emerginata*
	Serissa foetida
Weeping fig	*Ficus benjamina*
Yaupon holly	*Ilex vomitoria*

Some of these, such as the Weeping Fig and *Serissa foetida*, are great for beginners to practice the art of bonsai. All bonsai need to be well watered and must never be allowed to dry out. There are many books on the market that will serve as an introduction to the art of bonsai. If you receive a bonsai as a gift or buy a new one, find out its name and then gather all the information you need to care for it.

Experienced bonsai growers can plant tiny landscapes using bonsai, moss, rocks, and other undersized elements for an exquisite display.

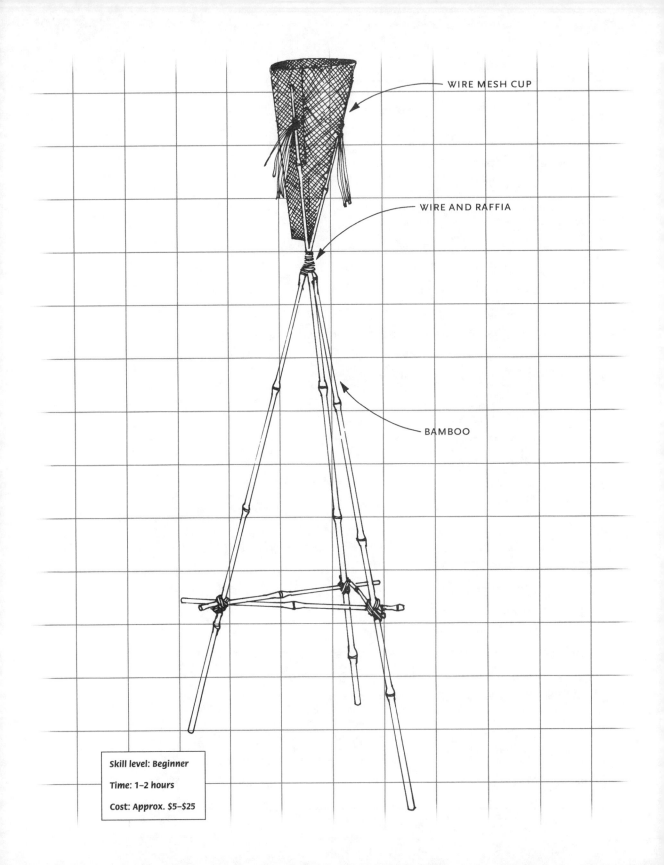

WIRE MESH CUP

WIRE AND RAFFIA

BAMBOO

Skill level: Beginner

Time: 1–2 hours

Cost: Approx. $5–$25

Bamboo and Raffia Plant Stand

B RING A TOUCH of the tropics to your
home! This simple design is elegant as well
as sturdy and makes a great place to keep a variety of showy plants. This stand can be built to fit
any plant and can be dismantled when the plant
has had its day.

Materials

- Four 4' lengths of bamboo (available at garden centers and hardware stores)
- 20-gauge galvanized wire
- One piece of fine wire mesh, at least 2' long
- Raffia (available at craft stores)

Tools

- Small saw
- Scissors
- Wire cutters

Method

1. Join three of the bamboo poles with wire approximately 10" from the top, so that they form a cup-shaped triangle at the top.
2. Cut three 16" lengths of bamboo from the remaining piece of bamboo.
3. Join each of the three bottom supports to the legs and each other with wire approximately 9" from the bottom.
4. Trim the mesh to form a conical cup that will hold a 4½" pot. Hold the mesh cone together with a couple of pieces of wire, threaded through the overlap.
5. Place the mesh cone inside the top of the bamboo supports and fasten it to the supports by threading wire around the bamboo and through the cone. Make sure that the mesh sits in the center of the bamboo supports.
6. Wrap the first joint of the bamboo with raffia and then wrap each of the bottom supports so that the wire is hidden.
7. Thread a few strands of raffia between the mesh cup and the bamboo supports where they are joined with the wire and make tassels on three sides of the mesh cup.

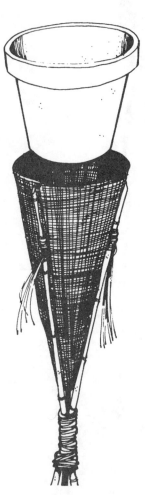

Figure 39-1

This plant stand looks great with moss lining the mesh cup and disguising the pot. Place moss on top of your pot as well to give it a lush appearance.

Figure 39-2

Part Five

Frames and Trellises

Frames and Trellises

Trellises combine form and function in innumerable creative ways. Frames, on the other hand, are all about form. Trellises often gain their interest from the materials from which they are made as well as the plants they support. Frames can be interesting objects in the garden in their own right.

The trellises in this section are very simple but can easily be adapted into far more complex and unique structures. The best way to make your trellis stand out is to make it out of a natural material. Twig or driftwood trellises (see pages 214 and 225) look wonderful in the garden. Consider using bamboo or even flexible copper tubing for the same purpose. The material used to help make climbing plants "stand" should complement their particular beauty. A copper trellis would look well supporting a robust climber with bright flowers. A twig trellis suits any number of unpretentious garden inhabitants, such as sweet peas or rambling rose. Driftwood, so unexpected yet natural in a garden, could be used to hold up almost anything, but looks best with plants reminiscent of the seashore.

Don't forget that you can use the basic trellis principles to build latticework. Rather than building two uprights and a graduated series of rungs, alter your proportions for a series of uprights and longer rungs. Once again, any number of materials other than milled lengths of wood will work to build latticework.

The topiary frames in this section are pure whimsy. Topiary is an ancient art associated with formal Roman gardens. The practice of forming trees and shrubs into unnatural forms has gone in and out of fashion ever since. Fanciful topiaries are particularly in vogue these days. Representational topiaries are the ones I enjoy most, although a well-shaped geometric tree also has its charms. I love nothing more than peering into a garden and discovering that someone has taken the time to shape a boxwood shrub into a fish. There is a childlike satisfaction and delight in such a discovery that always makes me feel I would be sure to like the person who created it.

Many people buy their topiary frames from a dealer. These are often simple frames for shaping trees into balls or concentric circles. Some companies provide more unusual forms such as dinosaurs and other creatures. You can also order custom-built soldered iron frames in the shapes of your choosing. And then again, you can make your own!

The frames in this book are made with chicken wire and heavy wire, soldered or wrapped at the joints. They are inexpensive and surprisingly simple to make. Best of all, they will get you started on customizing your own topiary frames, allowing your imagination to run wild.

Simple wire frames are great alternatives to commercial topiary frames because they can be formed into any shape you wish and they can be altered as necessary. For instance, if your boxwood simply refuses to grow in a direction needed to hide part of your frame, bend that part of the frame to bury it in the available leaves. Homemade wire frames allow you to train the shrub or plant to fit the frame, and also to adjust the frame to fit the plant. This flexibility is not possible with iron frames. Wire frames are very durable and surprisingly strong and should work for most small to medium topiary forms.

Chicken wire frames are most suitable for ivy. Because they are lightweight, they cannot be used to hold heavy plantings. If your frame won't support the weight of moss and ivy cuttings (the traditional way to plant an ivy topiary), you can place your frame in a tub, partially stuff it with moss, and train the ivy over the frame. Another option is to cut the frame open, place a pot right inside it, and train the ivy out and around the frame.

Chicken wire frames can also be left empty in the garden— rather like postmodern lawn art. At VanDusen Botanical Display Garden in Vancouver, a wonderful public garden, they hold an event each winter called the Festival of Lights. The entire garden is strung with lights and, walking through, one is transported into a sparkling fantasy world. The staff at VanDusen are highly skilled at garden decorations and each year the Festival of Lights includes examples of unplanted chicken wire frames. Rounding the corner you may come upon a tableaux of giant penguins, their hollow bodies strung with tiny white lights. Giant wire insects fly frozen overhead, and reindeer prance in the middle of a glowing red clearing. The creative possibilities for chicken wire frames are endless. And once you get started it may be hard to stop.

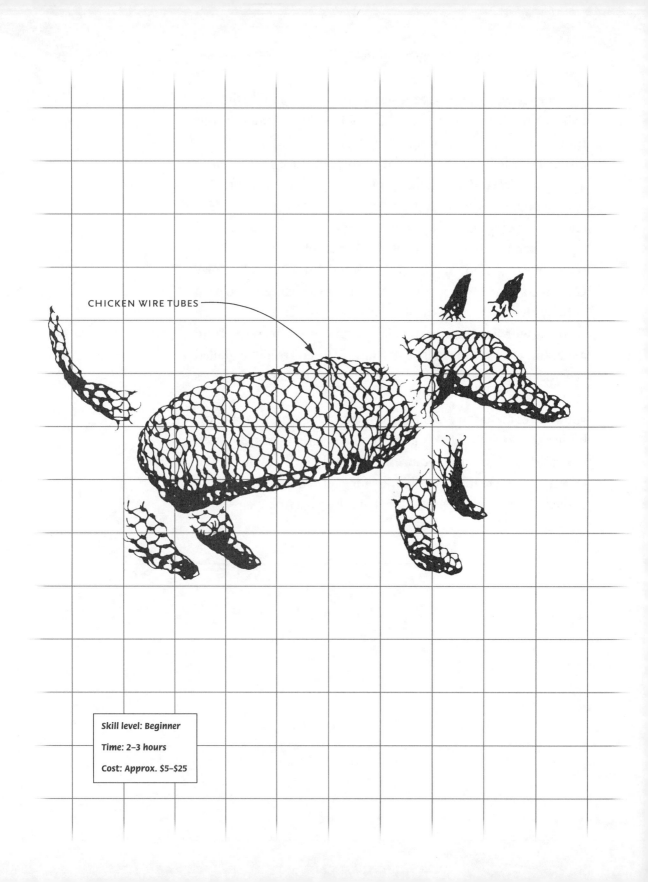

CHICKEN WIRE TUBES

Skill level: Beginner

Time: 2–3 hours

Cost: Approx. $5–$25

Topiary
Dog

T<small>HE</small> <small>CHARM</small> of topiary lies in the combination of creativity and discipline the forms represent. Once you become comfortable shaping chicken wire and joining the shapes to one another you will realize that the options for creating fanciful or classical figures are unlimited. The only caveat is that if you actually want to plant your topiary form the shapes must be able to support the plant. Remember that chicken wire topiary forms are more suitable for ivy than for trees. Chicken wire creatures also look wonderful left bare and placed in the garden like visiting sprites. Strung with tiny white lights, they can create a fantasyland in your winter or summer garden at night.

Materials
- 5' of chicken wire

Tools
- Pliers
- Wire cutters
- Work gloves
- Safety goggles

Method

1. Cut a length of chicken wire approximately 2' long and 2' wide. Fashion it into a tube shape and join it together using the cut ends of the wire. This will be the body of the dog (Figure 40-1).

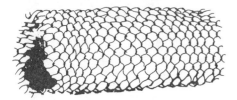

Figure 40-1

2. Making sure you are wearing your work gloves, use your hands to narrow one end of the dog's body slightly, so that it slopes down.

3. Cut another piece of chicken wire for the head, approximately 1' long and ½' wide. Bend this into a tube and fasten.

4. Narrow one end of the head until you have created a nose. Bend the wire in and down so the nose is enclosed. The bend should be fairly abrupt from the forehead to the nose so that the forehead is indicated in the shape.

5. Now, cut a piece of wire and bend it into a neck shape that fits the dog's body and head. The neck should have a bend in it and be narrower on the bottom.

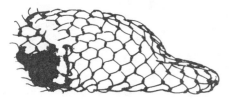

Figure 40-2

6. Cut four pieces of wire and shape them into legs. The front legs should be left longer and the closed ends shaped into paws. The back legs should have a bend fashioned into them. Cut an angle into the insides of the legs so that the legs fit onto the sides of

the dog. Fasten them on. You may need to trim the back legs to make them short enough to allow the dog to sit on its haunches.

7. Take two small pieces of chicken wire and fashion two ears that point up. This frame is a life sized model of one of my favorite dogs, a little blue heeler named Mike. Her long stout body, short sturdy legs, and big ears made her an ideal topiary candidate. I wish you luck if you want to create a whippet topiary!

8. Cut a length of chicken wire 6" long and shape it into a tail.

9. Shape the body of the dog so that the hindquarters are "closed" and the belly angles up, and then add the tail.

10. If you want to plant over top of your topiary canine, find a long tin container and plant it with any type of ivy (small-leafed varieties are best).

11. Cut a hole in the underside of the dog's behind and stuff the inside with as much moss as possible.

12. Place the dog in the ivy container and begin to train the ivy up and through the dog, so that eventually it is completely covered. Depending on the season and growing conditions, it can take three to six months to cover a frame. Water your dog often to keep the ivy happy and to keep the moss moist.

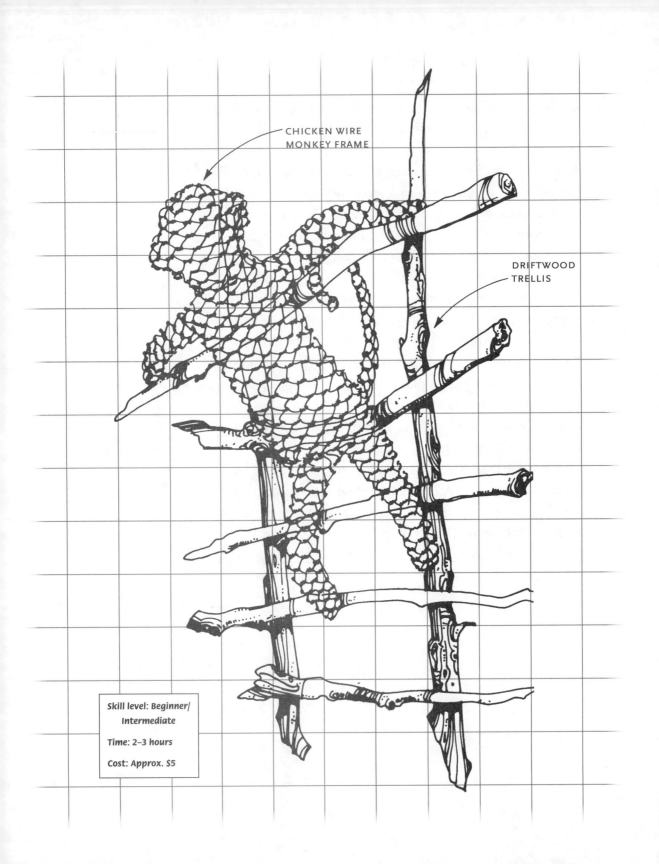

CHICKEN WIRE
MONKEY FRAME

DRIFTWOOD
TRELLIS

Skill level: Beginner/
Intermediate

Time: 2–3 hours

Cost: Approx. $5

Topiary
Monkey

Perched on a trellis and hung in a tree, this topiary monkey will delight onlookers. This topiary form is made using the same technique as the topiary dog on page 213. Build a twig or driftwood trellis to hold the monkey and further enhance the effect. Unusual accents, such as this monkey, will personalize your garden and lend it a sense of whimsy and fun.

Materials

- Approximately 5' of chicken wire
- Fine-gauge silver wire (wire mesh for monkey's muzzle)
- A piece of hardware cloth, at least 8" × 8"
- Two 3' lengths of driftwood
- Four 1½' lengths of driftwood
- 2½" screws
- One nail
- Large bag of moss
- One 12" pot of ivy
- Two 4"–6" pots of ivy

Tools

- Safety glasses
- Work gloves
- Wire cutters
- Hammer
- Electric drill

Method

1. Cut a 2¼' length of chicken wire and cut it 1¼' up the middle.
2. Form the single piece into the monkey's body and the cut lengths into the legs. You may want to trim the legs to make them appear tapered. Join the tube-shaped pieces using the cut ends of the chicken wire. If you need to reinforce the "seams," weave fine-gauge wire through both sides.
3. Form a length of chicken wire, approximately 9"–12" long, into a round head.
4. Fashion two arms from the chicken wire and a thinner tube for a tail (the tail should be longer than the arms).
5. Squeeze together the top of the monkey's body to suggest a neck, and join the head to the body.
6. Attach the arms and the tail.

7. Fashion two semicircular ears out of the chicken wire and attach them to the monkey's head.

8. Now, using your hands, shape the monkey's limbs into monkey-like positions (Figure 41-1). Manipulate the wire that makes up the head to emphasize the jaw and suggest a thick brow. If any piece of your monkey doesn't seem to look right, don't hesitate to remove it and trim or squeeze it with your hands into a more pleasing shape. One of the great things about working with chicken wire is that it is so flexible.

9. Build the driftwood trellis following the instructions for the Basic Trellis (see page 225), but instead using pilot hole and nail construction and an electric screwdriver (Figure 41-2).

10. Arrange the monkey so it sits perched on the trellis. Wire it securely to the trellis.

11. Cut open the back of the monkey and stuff the body so that it is lined with moss. Take the large ivy out of its pot and insert it into the monkey's body.

12. Stuff the monkey's arms, head, and tail with moss. Cut a hole in the monkey's head, take a small ivy out of its pot, and insert it into the head.

13. Train the ivy around the monkey's body, limbs, and head so that the plant winds around the arms, legs, and tail.

14. Cut the wire mesh into a circular piece, and shape it into a cup to form the monkey's muzzle. Stuff the muzzle with moss and wire it to the monkey's head.

15. Hang the monkey and its trellis in a tree or on a garden wall and sit back to enjoy your guest's reactions.

16. Make sure to water the ivy monkey frequently and continue to train the ivy around the body as it grows.

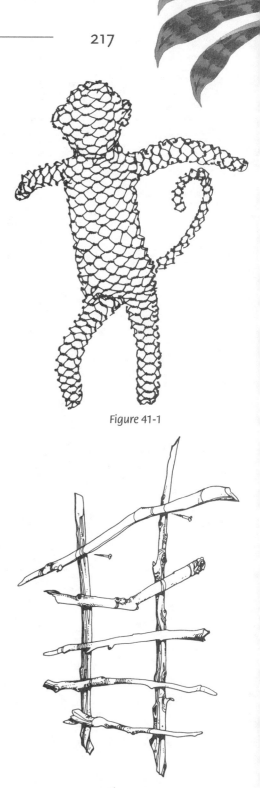

Figure 41-1

Figure 41-2

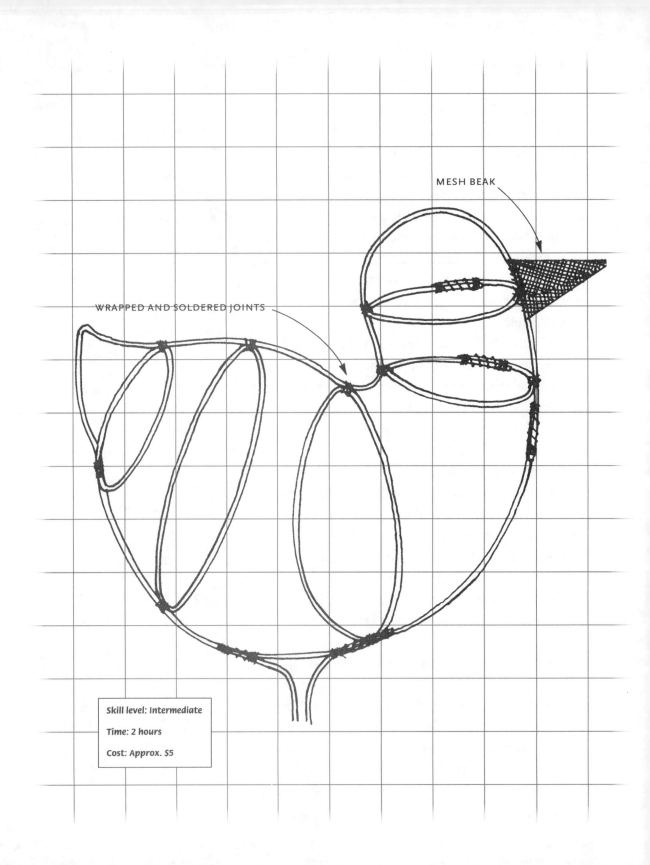

MESH BEAK

WRAPPED AND SOLDERED JOINTS

Skill level: Intermediate

Time: 2 hours

Cost: Approx. $5

Topiary
Chicken

T‍HIS FRAME is made from heavy wire and used to form trees and shrubs into topiary. You can clip evergreen topiaries into shapes without using a frame, but the frame will make clipping simpler and gives you something to tie branches to. Wire topiary forms can be soldered or wrapped at the joints or both. I wrapped and soldered this frame but if the wrapping is done carefully it would certainly suffice.

219

Materials

- 14-gauge wire (for the frame)
- 18-gauge wire (for wrapping the frame)
- Acid flux (if you are going to solder the joints of the frame)
- Solder

Tools

- Wire cutters
- Safety glasses
- Work gloves
- Flux brush
- Soldering iron with pencil tip
- Clean rags

Method

1. Fashion the 14-gauge wire into the shape of a chicken (see page 218). Wrap the wire so it overlaps where the tail forms with 18-gauge wire.
2. Form five circles from the 14-gauge wire so they will fit through the belly and neck, making the form three-dimensional. Join each circle where the wire overlaps with 18-gauge wire.
3. One at a time, join each of the circles to the frame of the chicken, wrapping them top and bottom with 18-gauge wire. Add a stake made of a doubled piece of 14-gauge wire attached to the frame at the bottom.
4. If you desire, you can then solder the joints where the circles attach to the frame. To begin, place the frame on a fire-retardant surface. If you are working outside, make sure the wind is not blowing strongly or you won't be able to see the flame tip on the soldering iron. Make sure your work surface has nothing that can catch fire on or around

it, and also be certain to keep a fire extinguisher handy. It is imperative that you wear safety glasses suitable for soldering. Secure the frame with clamps or some other non-flammable stabilizer so that it can't move while you are working on it. You may need to adjust it to reach some of the joints.

5. To solder the joints, rub them with a clean rag to remove any oil from your hands. Use the flux brush to paint flux into the joint.

6. Making sure you are wearing your glasses and fire-retardant work gloves, light the soldering iron so that the flame tip is on low and heat the joint until it glows red-hot.

7. Roll out enough solder so that you can touch an end to the hot joint. The solder should melt into the joint and harden almost instantly. Do not touch the soldered joint until it has cooled! Any solder that drips onto your work surface should scrape off easily.

8. Roll a piece of mesh into a cone and attach to the head to serve as a beak, fastening it with wire to keep it closed.

9. To plant the frame, choose an evergreen shrub, such as boxwood, and place the frame into the soil over the shrub. Trim the plant around the frame, tying branches to the frame as neccessary to help create the shape. Clip starting from the top of the shape and work your way down. When the bush has reached maturity and is in the shape you want, it should be clipped approximately twice a year.

Plant Suggestions

For an evergreen topiary, you should choose a plant that produces a lot of small leaves close together, such as one of the boxwood varieties or yew.

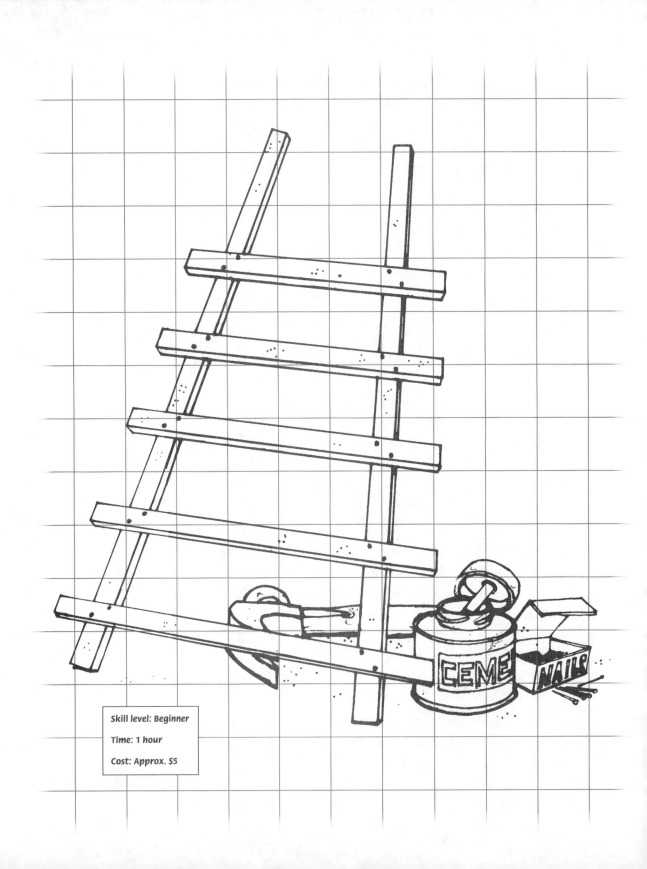

Skill level: Beginner

Time: 1 hour

Cost: Approx. $5

Basic
Trellis

THIS VERY SIMPLE trellis can be adjusted to suit any taste and size of plant. Consider building it with twigs, driftwood, or bamboo for a different effect.

Materials
- Approximately 10' of ½" × ½" wood
- Handful of small nails (brads)
- #100 grit sandpaper
- Rubber cement glue

Tools
- Handsaw
- Hammer
- Drill (optional)

Method
1. Cut two 24" upright pieces.
2. Cut one 15½" piece for the top rung. Cut one 14" piece, one 13" piece, one 11½" piece, and one 10½" piece.
3. Lay out the uprights.
4. Approximately 7"–8" from the bottom, add the bottom rung so there is a ⅞" overhang. Glue on the bottom rung with rubber cement and then nail it to the uprights.
5. At 3" intervals, glue and nail the rest of the rungs, leaving a ⅞" overhang on each side.
6. Sand the tops and sides of the uprights and rungs.

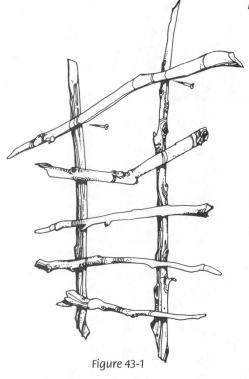

Figure 43-1

Plant Suggestions

This trellis is quite small and so is most suitable for slow-growing or small plants such as heart-leaf philodendron, miniature rose, grape ivy, or English ivy.

Twig Trellis

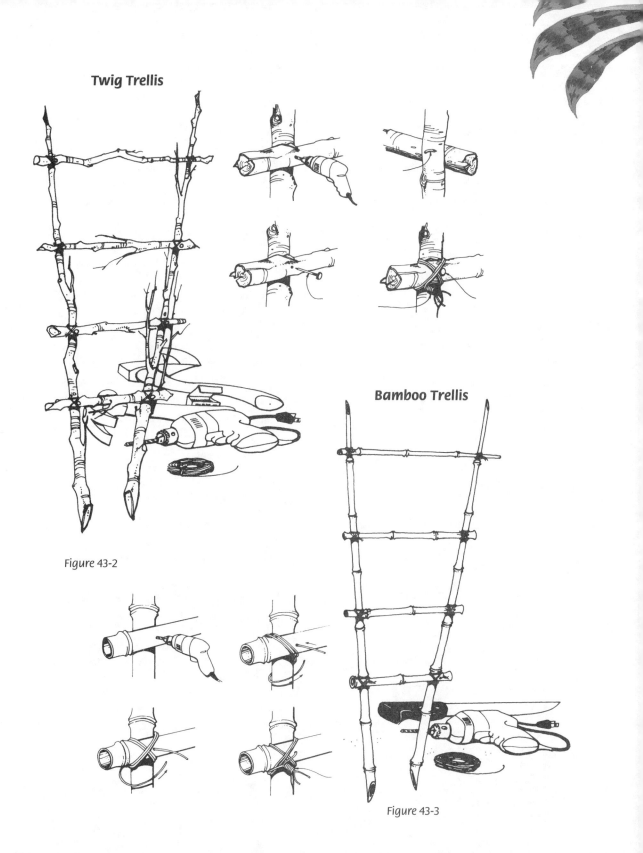

Figure 43-2

Bamboo Trellis

Figure 43-3

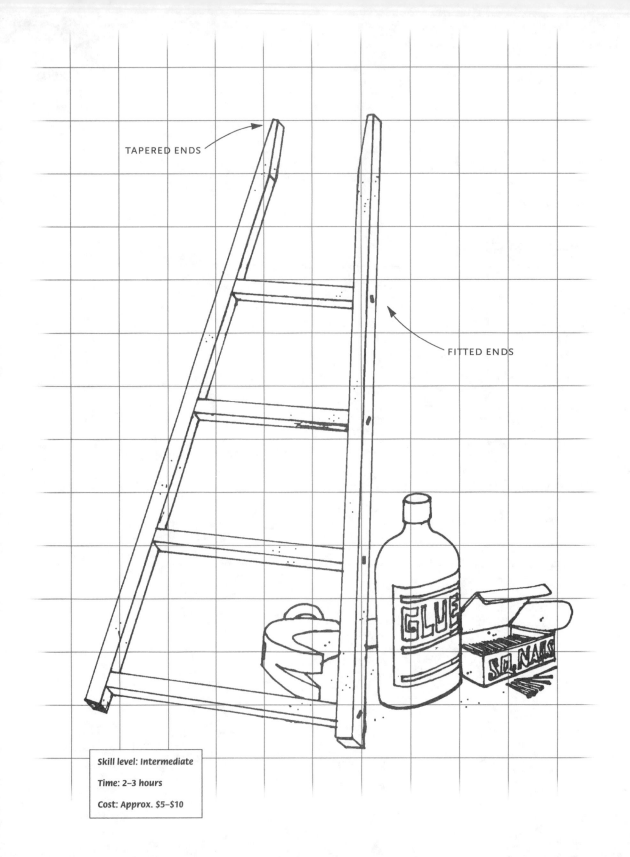

TAPERED ENDS

FITTED ENDS

Skill level: Intermediate

Time: 2–3 hours

Cost: Approx. $5–$10

Redwood Trellis

THE REDWOOD TRELLIS is a simple and classic project for displaying your creeping or climbing plants. It differs from the basic trellis with its fitted rungs. Put it in a large pot or lean it up against a wall in the garden.

Materials

- Approximately 8' of ½" × ½" redwood
- Wood glue
- Square cut brads

Tools

- Handsaw and sliding bevel (or table saw)
- Hammer

Method

1. Cut two 28" upright pieces.
2. Cut one 5½" piece for the bottom and angle the ends. Place the bottom piece between the uprights and adjust the ends as necessary so that they fit exactly between the uprights.
3. Once the bottom rung has been cut and angled, the rest of the pieces are easy. Cut one 7½" long piece, one 9¾" piece, and one 12½" piece.
4. Set the two uprights on a flat surface, such as a workbench, and fit the bottom rung between them. Cut the ends of the rest of the rungs to match the angle of the bottom rung, and slide them between the uprights so that they fit snugly. You may need to trim them to adjust the angles.
5. Once all the pieces are cut and angled to fit inside the uprights, dab glue onto the bottom rung and squeeze it between the uprights, making sure it is level. Glue each of the rungs in the same way.
6. Once the glue has dried (follow the instructions for drying times), set the trellis on its side and drive a brad through the uprights into the rungs. Square cut brads will prevent the wood from splitting.

Climbing Plants

Small or Slow-Growing Climbers

	Dipladenia sanderi rosia
Cape leadwort	*Plumbago auriculata*
Cape Ivy, Wax vine	*Senecio macroglossus*
German Ivy	*Senecio mikanioides*
Grape ivy	*Cissus chombifolia*
	Cissus striata

Other Climbers

(Note: These can be pinched back or your trellis can be built to fit the full size that plant will eventually reach.)

Bittersweet	*Celastus scandens*
Bittersweet Oriental	*C elastus orbiculatus*
Boston ivy	*Parthenocissus tricuspidata*
Evergreen	*Clematis armandi* or
	Clematis montana
Grapevine	*Vitis coignetiae*
Hops	*Humulus lupulus*
Honeysuckle	*Lonicera x americana*
Hydrangea, climbing	*Hydrangea anomala*
'Lalandei'	*Pyracantha coccinea*
'Nelly Moser'	*Clematis*
Ornamental quince	*Chaenomeles speciosa*
Scotch flame flower	*Trapaeolum speciosum*
Passion vine	*Passiflora caerulea*
'Royal Gold'	*Rosa*
Trumpet vine	*Campsis radicans*
Virginia creeper	*Parthenocissus quinquefolia*
Wisteria	

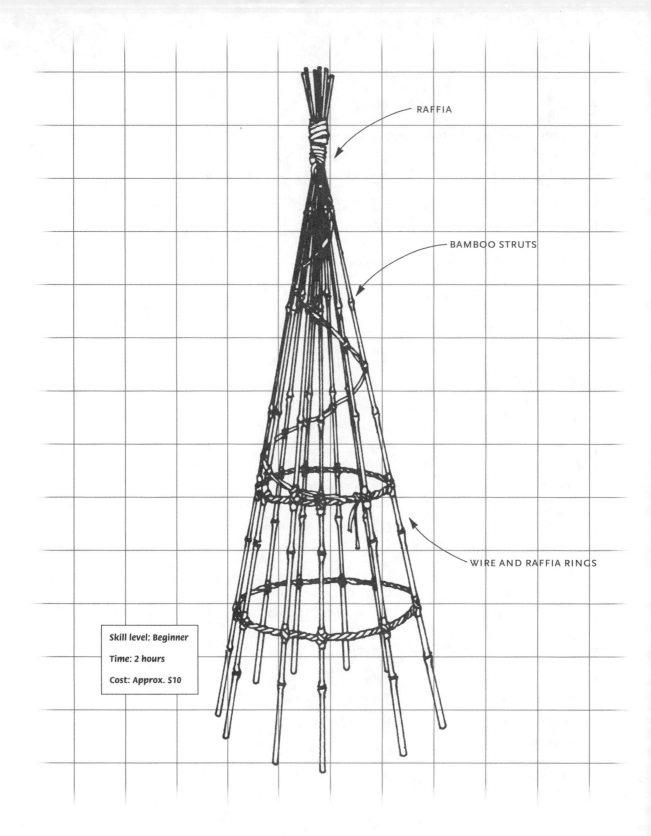

RAFFIA

BAMBOO STRUTS

WIRE AND RAFFIA RINGS

Skill level: Beginner

Time: 2 hours

Cost: Approx. $10

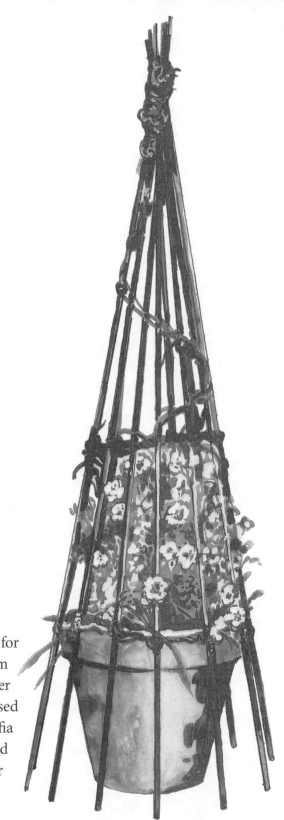

Project 45

Bamboo
Teepee
Trellis

THE BAMBOO Teepee Trellis is ideal for
a dramatic display in the living room
or outdoors. Simple to build, you can alter
the size to suit any room or space. I used
dyed green bamboo and dark green raffia
for this project. It makes an unusual and
elegant accent in any room with ivy or
miniature roses trained up it.

231

Materials

- 11 bamboo canes
- 20-gauge galvanized wire
- 16-gauge galvanized wire
- Hemp or raffia
- Large pot

Tools

- Handsaw
- Wire cutters
- Scissors
- Work gloves

Method

1. Arrange the bamboo around a large pot and secure it at the top with 20-gauge wire so it forms a teepee shape. It may be helpful to get someone to help you hold the bamboo still for this step and the next.

Figure 45-1

2. With your helper holding the top securely, wrap the pieces of bamboo with 20-gauge wire just below the lip of the pot so that you form a ring to keep the bamboo in a circular shape around the pot.

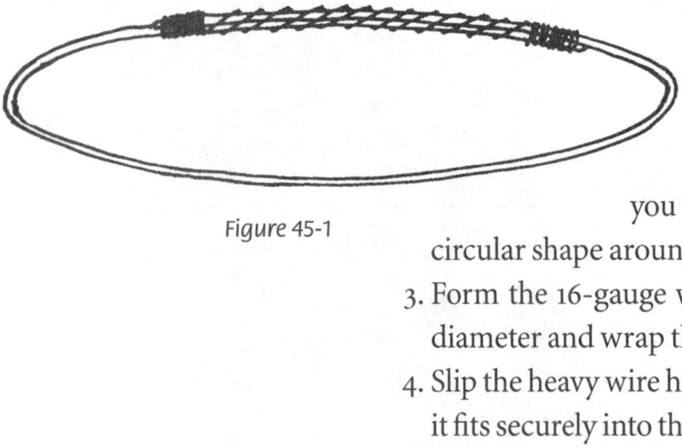

3. Form the 16-gauge wire into a circle approximately 8" in diameter and wrap the ends to secure them (Figure 45-1).

4. Slip the heavy wire hoop into the trellis form and slide it so it fits securely into the circle formed by the bamboo. Fasten it to the trellis by wrapping the hoop and the bamboo with 20-gauge wire (Figure 45-2).

5. Wrap the bottom, middle, and top of the trellis with raffia. Wrap the raffia around the wire hoops and then around the bamboo struts (Figures 45-3 to 45-5).

6. For added interest, wrap raffia at a diagonal down the first half of the trellis as shown.

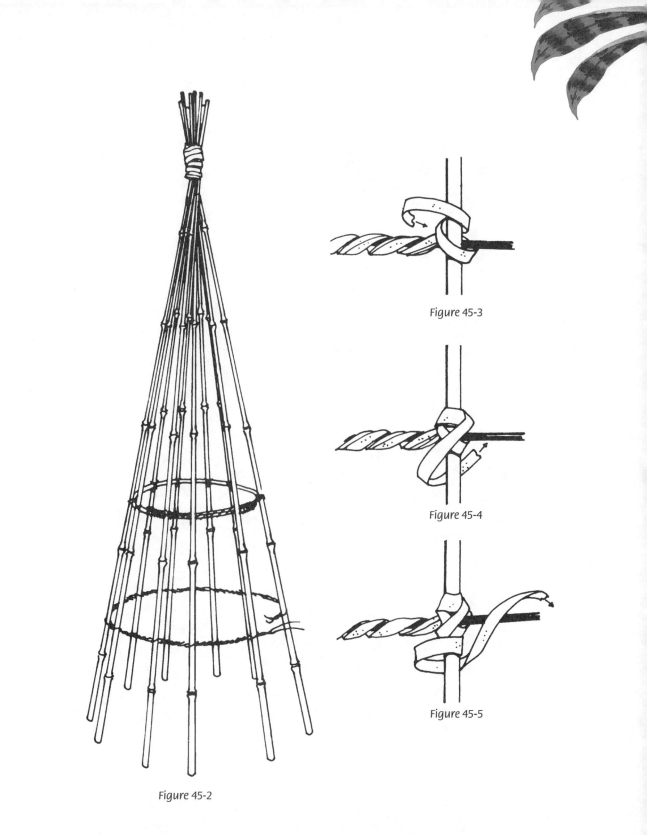

Figure 45-2

Figure 45-3

Figure 45-4

Figure 45-5

Part Six

Pots and
More Pots

Pots and More Pots

POTS COME in every shape and size and in materials ranging from plastic to clay. Clay pots appeal to some gardeners and plastic to others. In this section we focus on some of the creative possibilities with clay pots.

Plastic pots are the favorites of many indoor gardeners. Lightweight compared to clay, they come in a variety of styles designed to make watering easier and more effective. One particular favorite is the enclosed plastic pot with the built-in hole for watering. The pot looks after drainage and ensures no messes from overflow watering. Plastic pots used to come only in a very small assortment of colors: black, dark green, and white. There are more colors to choose from now, and some plastic pots are even made to look like stone or clay. If you prefer plastic pots, but don't like the available colors, you can paint them just as you would clay. They will also take faux finishes. Many plastic pots have a texture on the outside which you will not be able to disguise, but it shouldn't detract from the overall appearance of your pot.

Clay pots are the old-fashioned standard among gardeners. They are very inexpensive, particularly in the smaller sizes. Left untreated or painted, clay pots breathe because they are porous. They also age nicely. Even mildew looks great on a clay pot. And clay takes paint very nicely, allowing you to create wonderful effects. On the downside, clay is heavy, especially when it gets wet, and it is breakable. After clay has been painted, it should be sealed with a waterproof polyurethane. If your plants are of the variety that like containers that "breathe," you can still paint your clay pots. Just don't put a full coat of paint on them or seal them. Instead, paint on designs, leaving the rest of the surface natural.

A popular decorating trick is to paint a collection of clay pots and place them on a shelf or around a room. They needn't even contain plants to look great. Painted pots make an attractive display in their own right. Perhaps if you have a bit of a black thumb, you can pretend you're a gardener and decorate a few clay pots. Tell friends that the plants are next. You're just working up to them!

Painted clay pots look great in groups. Vary the height and sizes and use complementary finishes to create eye-catching collections. I like to paint several pots in contrasting colors and then add a clear or pearlescent glaze. Another idea is to develop a few similar designs (copy them from books or cards or other sources), turn the designs into stencils, and using alternating colors, stencil several pots. For instance, paint one pot white with a gold rim. Stencil a beetle in forest green several times along the body. Take a second pot and paint it green with a white rim. Stencil a dragonfly along the body of the pot in gold. Continue using different variations of the same colors and stencils until you have created a terra cotta collection that will make an intriguing display for any corner.

In this section you will learn how to crackle (create a network of cracks in paint), as well as stencil, decoupage, gold-leaf, and mosaic, and will be given an assortment of great patterns that you can stencil on pots. Don't stop with these projects. Learn these techniques and combine them in new ways. Turn your plant pots into artwork.

Tips on Clay Pots

- If you are going to paint the entire surface of your clay pot, make sure you seal every part of the pot, including the drainage hole at the bottom, with a polyurethane sealer.

- Never overwinter clay pots outside in cold weather. Store them in a shed or the basement during the winter instead.

- Before you plant your pots again in the spring, soak them in a bath of 1 part bleach to 5 parts water and then scrub them clean. Let them dry. This will kill any bacteria that linger in the porous material.

- If you want to use your clay pot as a container, or use it to cover the original plastic pot, make sure the outer clay pot is at least an inch wider and taller than the pot it is to hide.

- To increase humidity and moisture around a plant, pack the space between the pots with damp moss.

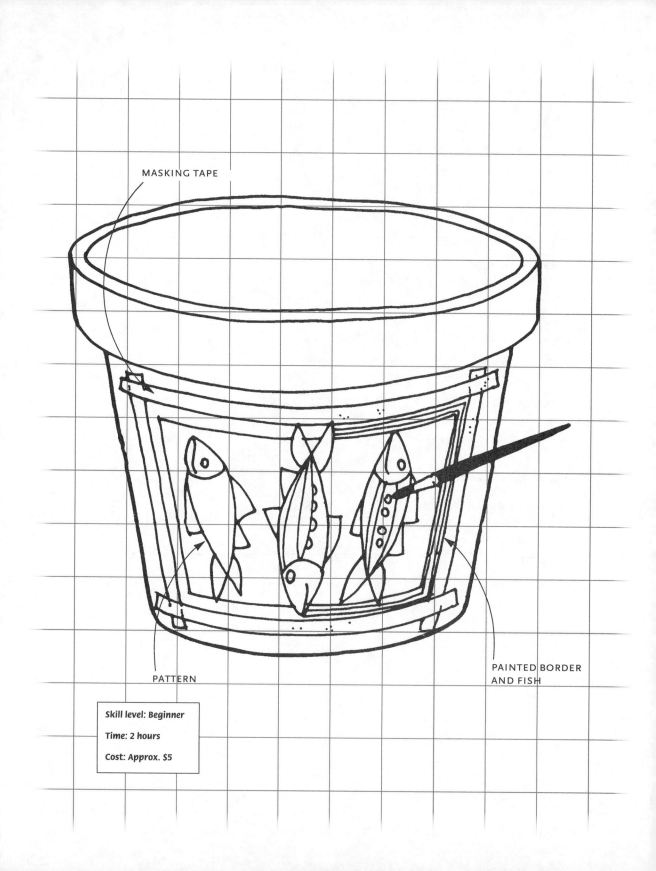

MASKING TAPE

PATTERN

PAINTED BORDER
AND FISH

Skill level: Beginner

Time: 2 hours

Cost: Approx. $5

Project 46

Freehand and Traced Designs

Freehand painting on a clay pot can be very rewarding and produce excellent results, even if you don't feel yourself to be a "talented artist." Clay pots are inexpensive and take paint very well and if you choose the right images, precision matters little. Find an image you like that you feel would be possible for you to copy. Greeting cards, postcards, and wrapping paper are good sources for inspiration. Practice copying the images as closely as you can, in pencil, on a clean piece of paper. When you are confident that you can reproduce what you see, copy it lightly onto your clay pot in pencil, erasing when necessary.

Then just follow the lines to paint in the image. Embellish or simplify the pattern or picture as you desire.

If you want to avoid freehand painting, you can trace the pattern or image onto your pot with graphite paper. Simply affix the pattern onto the pot in a few places with

241

masking tape. Slide the piece of graphite paper underneath, chalky side to the pot. Trace over the pattern, then remove it and the graphite paper. The outlines will be left in chalk on the pot. You can make your own graphite paper by rubbing a piece of chalk all over the rough side of a piece of brown paper. You can also trace around the pattern or image on its reverse side, attach it to the pot, and then retrace it on the right side.

These fish were painted freehand using acrylic paint. The design was based loosely on a postcard. Feel free to use the pattern provided to recreate them or try your hand at another image of your choosing.

Fish Pattern

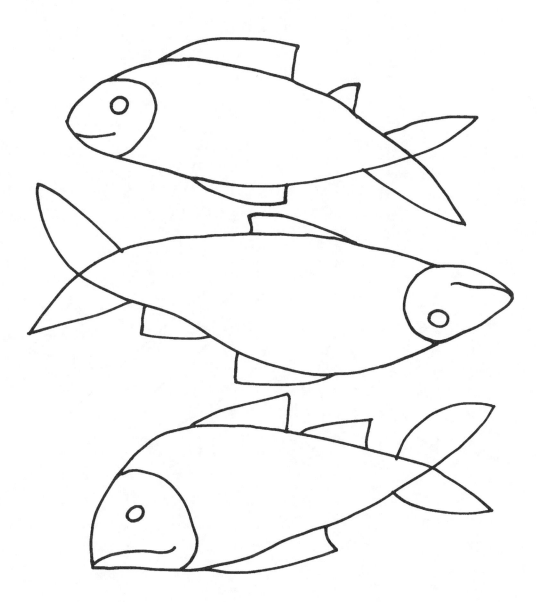

Beetle Pattern

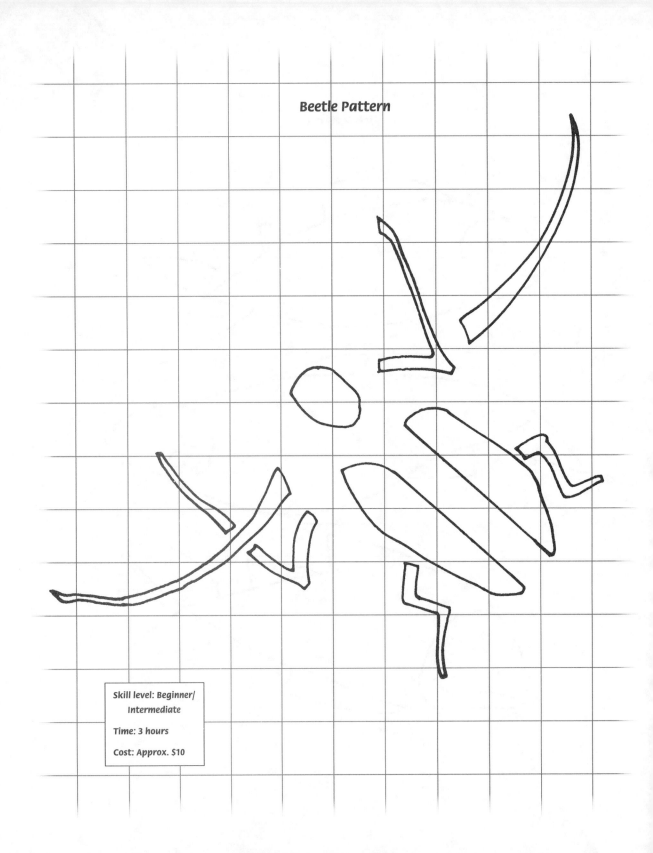

Skill level: Beginner/
Intermediate

Time: 3 hours

Cost: Approx. $10

Crackled
and Stenciled
Pot

CRACKLING IS a beautiful faux finish for clay pots, as it enhances their classically aged look. Combining crackling and simple stenciling, as was done here, is a winning combination that will allow you to inexpensively create pots that would be much more costly if purchased in a store. You can also customize the look of your plant displays with a stenciled motif of your own making.

Materials
- Light-colored acrylic paint
- Dark acrylic paint (cream and dark green work very well for this project)
- Metallic gold or bronze acrylic paint
- Crackling medium
- Brown paper (butcher's paper)
- Repositionable spray adhesive
- Clay pot (this project uses an octagonal pot)
- Polyurethane spray

Tools
- Several paintbrushes
- Scissors
- Utility knife
- Face mask

Method
1. Paint the pot with a dark-colored base coat. Let it dry.
2. Paint a thick coat of crackling medium on top of the base coat and let it dry.
3. To make the paint crackle, paint over the layer of clear crackling medium with light-colored acrylic paint. The instructions for the crackling medium often suggest painting over the crackle layer within two to four hours, but I have had greater success after five hours or more. Do not overlap the third coat. Carefully paint on even strokes to achieve a web of cracks in the paint. Let the paint dry thoroughly overnight.
4. Find an image to stencil. You can buy a small stencil from a hobby or paint store, draw your own, or trace one from a stenciling book. Feel free to use the stencil provided here.
5. Trace out the stencil at the desired size onto brown paper.
6. Cut around the traced image with a utility knife or scissors.

7. Spray the shiny side of the brown paper with repositionable spray adhesive and affix it to the crackled pot where you want the image to appear.

8. Dab your brush into a bit of acrylic paint and then offload most of the paint onto a paper towel. When the paint comes off the brush very lightly and evenly, rub the brush over the open area of the stencil until the image is the color you desire. Make sure the edges of the stencil are firmly attached to the pot so the paint doesn't bleed under the paper.

9. Repeat as desired.

10. Rub the lip of the pot with a metallic paint so it appears to be aged.

11. When the stencils are dry, coat the entire pot, inside and out, with polyurethane spray and let it dry.

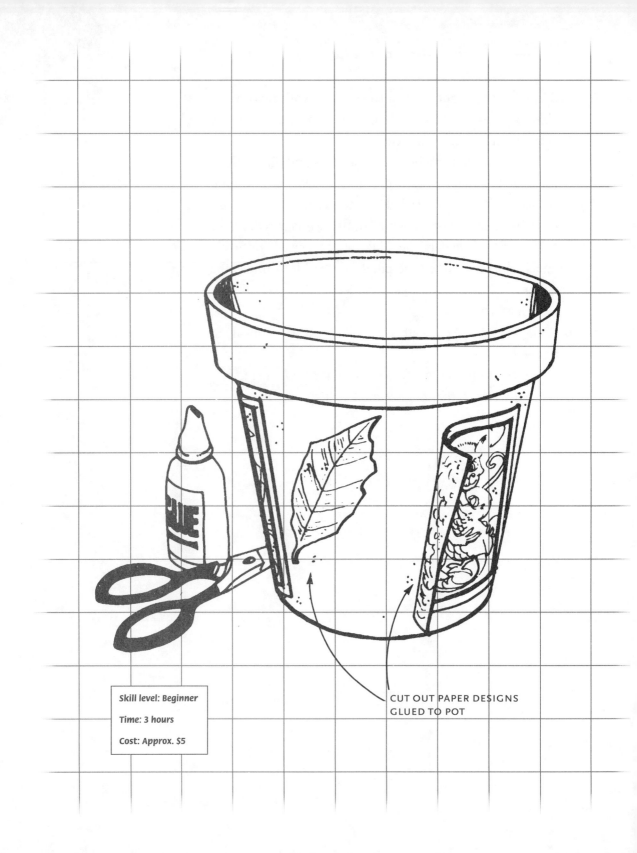

Skill level: *Beginner*

Time: **3 hours**

Cost: **Approx. $5**

CUT OUT PAPER DESIGNS
GLUED TO POT

Decoupage Pot

T HE BEAUTY of decoupage is that you, armed only with glue and scissors, can produce great works of art. All you need is an eye for an attractive picture and you are set! Decoupage is an old faux finishing technique that works brilliantly with clay pots. Combine images from different sources to create pots that will dazzle. Line up your empty decoupaged pots along a windowsill, or plant them with matching plants. A set of matched decoupage pots covered in seed packets and planted with small herb topiary will amuse and delight.

Materials

- Images on paper
- Glue
- Decoupage medium
- Acrylic paint (for a background color)

Tools

- Scissors (use cuticle scissors for very small pieces)
- Paintbrushes (at least two)
- Fine steel wool or sandpaper

Method

1. Paint the pot with a heavy coat of acrylic paint in the desired color. Let it dry.
2. Cut out your paper images using scissors. Angle the scissors away from the print for a sharper edge.
3. Glue the images to the pot after positioning them to see where they look best. Press the images onto the pot and smooth out all the air pockets underneath so they lie completely flat. A barely moistened sponge may help smooth the images neatly onto the surface of the pot. Allow the glue to dry completely.
4. Brush on a layer of decoupage medium. Your strokes should go only one way. Work slowly and carefully to minimize the foamy bubbles that may appear in the decoupage medium.
5. Allow the first layer to dry. Add as many layers as necessary to give the impression that the cutouts have been hand-painted or inlaid on the pot.
6. When the decoupage medium is level with the cutouts (the surface of the pot is entirely smooth), lightly sand the surface with steel wool or very fine sandpaper.

Sources for Images

- Wrapping paper
- Magazines
- Cards
- Photographs
- Newspapers
- Books (color photocopies of pages)
- Packaging, such as labels and wrapping
- Menus
- Stamps
- Decorative paper

See page 51 for a selection of possible decoupage images.

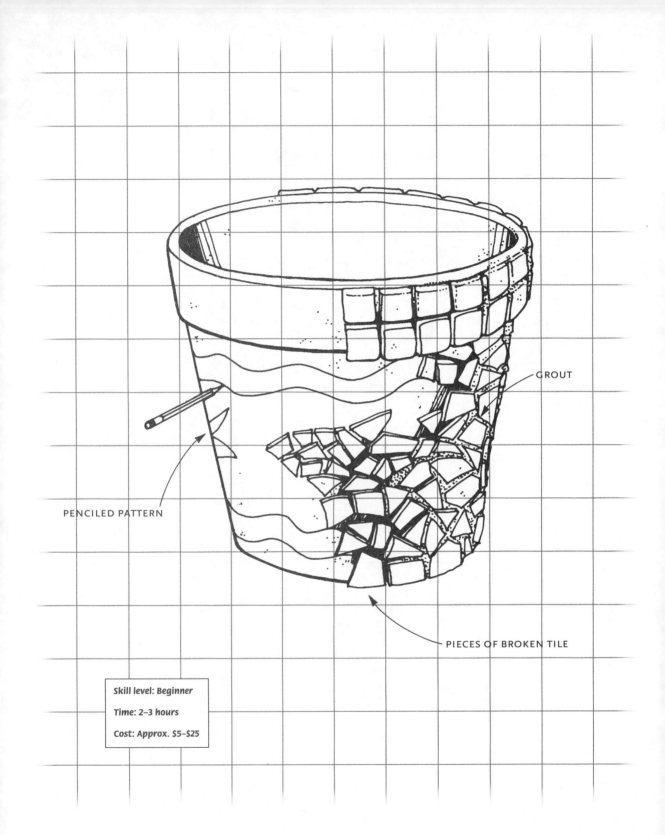

GROUT

PENCILED PATTERN

PIECES OF BROKEN TILE

Skill level: Beginner

Time: 2–3 hours

Cost: Approx. $5–$25

Project 49

Mosaic
Pot

A POT COVERED with mosaic will bring an old-fashioned charm to any décor. The added weight of the ceramic and grout makes mosaic an ideal finish for pots that hold top-heavy plants, such as topiary trees. The ceramics you choose to cover your pot and the pattern they follow will determine the overall look of the pot. The blue and white fish design on this pot echoes classic dinnerware patterns that many people keep for everyday use.

Materials
- Enough 3" × 3" tiles to cover the pot (approximately 14 tiles for a pot 12" across)
- Enough 1" × 1" tiles to cover the rim of the pot (tiles are available at hardware and tile shops)
- Tile adhesive
- Sanded tile grout
- Acrylic paint (if you want to paint plain white tiles)
- Pencil
- Polyurethane spray

Tools
- Hammer
- Safety glasses
- Work gloves
- Latex gloves
- Rags
- Palette knife
- Face mask

Method
1. Mark out the desired design on your pot with a pencil.
2. If you bought white tiles, paint them the desired colors using acrylic paint.
3. Wearing your safety glasses and work gloves, use the hammer to break up the large tiles so that they are approximately the same size. The hammer will chip the paint off the tiles, but these chipped spots can be touched up later.
4. Using tile adhesive, glue the 1" square tiles around the rim of the pot.
5. Following the pattern you have drawn, glue the tile pieces onto the pot with tile adhesive. Let them dry for 24 hours.
6. Mix up the grout and spread it between the cracks in the tiles, wiping off the excess with a rag as you proceed.

7. Allow the grout to set for approximately 10 minutes, then use the rag to clean the residue off the tiles. Let the grout dry for another half-hour or so, then wipe the tiles again, this time with a damp rag.

8. Now if you want to touch up or add to the paint on the tile, you can do so. Let the paint dry.

9. Allow the entire pot to dry for three days and then spray with a coat of polyurethane finish.

Mosaic pots look wonderful planted with trees trained into topiary standards. Information on training tree standards can be found on page 126. Another way to enhance the look of your mosaic pot is to add a layer of round river rocks in a circular pattern around the plant on top of the soil surface. Rocks not only accentuate the mosaic texture, but also serve to keep the soil moist. River rocks can be found, as their name implies, on the banks of rivers, and also at some garden centers.

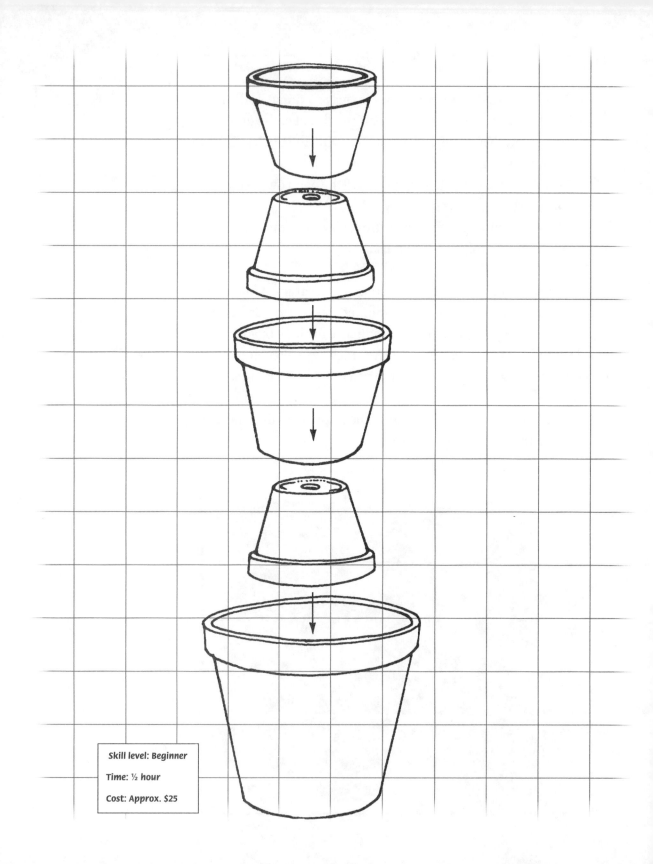

Skill level: Beginner

Time: ½ hour

Cost: Approx. $25

Stacked Pot Planter

STACKED POT planters are an inexpensive way to create a lay-ered and tiered plant display. A Stacked Pot Planter will allow you to combine a variety of plants that complement one another for a sophisticated effect. Very simple to assemble, the stacked planter gains its impact from your choice of plants. Make sure to choose plants with varying heights and leaf shapes. You can paint your stacked pots to add more interest to the display. A Stacked Pot Planter can be made in a large or small size, depending on where you want to place it. It can be used indoors or out, and go up several levels, if you like.

Materials

- One large clay pot
- One medium clay pot
- Three smaller clay pots that will fit comfortably, upside down, inside the large and medium pots
- A collection of plants to fill the lower, middle, and upper tiers
- Moss
- Soil

Method

1. Flip a small pot upside down and place it inside the large pot.
2. Place the medium pot, right side up, on top of the small pot, so that it protrudes above the large pot.
3. Place another small pot, upside down, inside the medium pot.
4. Place the third small pot, right side up, on top of the second small pot.
5. Fill the lower tier around the inverted small pot with a layer of soil. Plant trailing and short plants in the lower tier.
6. Fill the second tier in the same way.
7. Plant a large or a few small plants of varying heights in the small top pot.

Plants for Stacked Pots

Variegated ivy	Hedera helix
Golden pothos	Scindapsus aureus
Asparagus/Emerald Fern	Asparagus densiflorus sprengeri
Wandering Jew	Zebrina pendula
Krinkle curl	Hoya carnosa
Spider plant	Chlorophytum comosum

Part Seven

Gardening Indoors
with Lights

Gardening Indoors
with Lights

FABULOUS INDOOR gardens are possible even if you have limited or nonexistent light available from windows. Plants can flourish in inauspicious circumstances if they are provided with sufficient artificial light. Lighting options for indoor gardeners are greater than ever before due to the advances made in fluorescent lights.

The standard bulbs found in most homes are incandescents. These light bulbs are not effective for indoor gardening because their color range is wrong for plants, much of their energy is given off as heat, and they emit fewer lumens per watt than fluorescents. Lumens is a measure of the visible light given off by a lamp. The greater the intensity of light output (the more lumens), the better for plants. Lumens are more important than color or spectrum, which is why standard fluorescent lights are as useful in indoor light gardening as specially designed plant lights.

The other measurement used for indoor gardening lights is footcandles. Footcandles refers to the amount of light striking an object. Footcandles are decreased as the light source moves further from the object, which means that a light with a high lumen output can be placed further from an object than one with a low lumen output.

Standard fluorescent lights used to be the best choice for indoor gardeners. They are energy efficient and their light covers a greater color spectrum than incandescents, which is important for plants. Their most serious drawback was that they were only available in tubes and odd shapes.

Compact fluorescents are the next generation of fluorescent lighting. Compact fluorescents are extremely energy efficient and they come in standard bulb shapes with a screw-in base. Early problems with compact fluorescents, such as low lumens output, flickering, and humming noises have been solved, and they now provide great opportunities for the indoor gardener. They can be used in banks of overhead tubes (as with standard fluorescents), as spotlights, or in combinations, depending on the needs of your plants and your indoor gardening space.

The light needs of plants differ. Low-light foliage plants can survive with 50 to 300 footcandles. To give you a sense of context, this means that these plants could survive in a regular office building with overhead fluorescent lighting. Flowering plants need at least 400 footcandles, and high-light plants need up to 1,000 footcandles. Your plants will need at least 16 hours of light each day.

The key to success with indoor light gardening is experimentation with the light sources. Remember that the effectiveness of your lights is reduced the further they are from the plants. For this reason, the lower portions of tall plants may suffer. One way to address this is to use a combination of overhead and spot lighting. Some plants cannot abide heat and so must be kept well away from warm or hot lights, while others won't be bothered at all.

Bright sunlight provides a plant with 10,000 footcandles of light and covers a very wide area. Artificial lights, on the other hand, only cover the length of the tube plus 3" on each side, or 3" wider than the circumference of the bulb. This means that you have to make sure your lights are trained as directly on your plants as possible and you may need multiple lights.

Indoor light gardens can be placed in enclosures such as aquariums or they can be placed under shelves (in order to hide

the lights), or lights can be added to the ceiling to create banks of fluorescent tubes. Tubes or bulbs can be suspended over plants, or bulbs can be used to spotlight plants using wall attachments.

Using modern light fixtures and home details such as shelving units, you can create indoor light arrangements that look very attractive. Once you have decided what plants you want to grow and where, you can arrange your lights. By combining bulbs and tubes in the wide array of available fixtures, you can achieve almost any effect and grow most plants.

Many people live in low-light conditions, but that doesn't mean that you cannot enjoy the life and beauty plants bring to a home. Indoor light gardening will allow you to customize your own personal plant place and grow those plants you thought were reserved only for people lucky enough to live in light-filled homes.

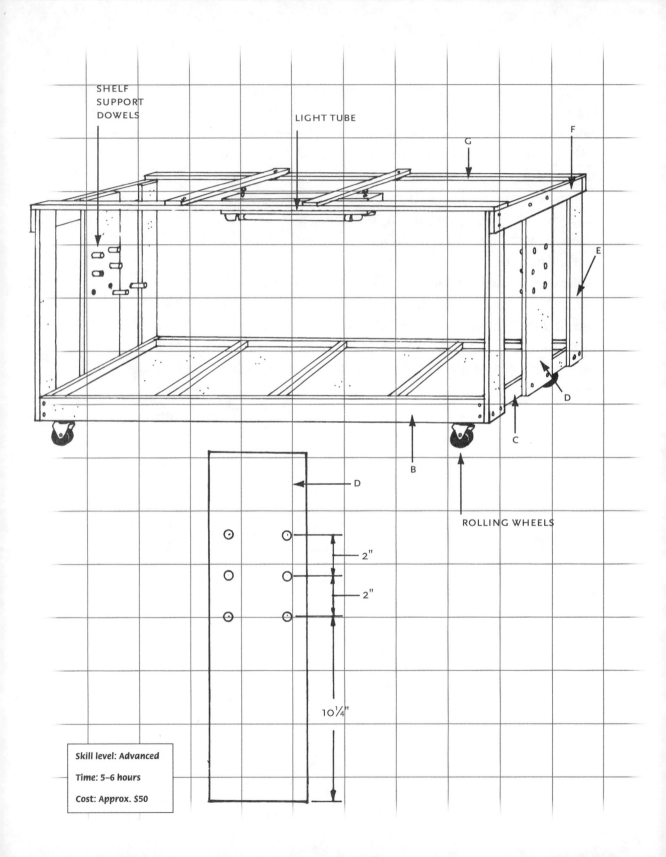

SHELF
SUPPORT
DOWELS

LIGHT TUBE

G

F

E

D

C

B

ROLLING WHEELS

D

2"

2"

10¼"

Skill level: Advanced

Time: 5–6 hours

Cost: Approx. $50

Design by Scott Banta

Rolling Light Tray for Seedlings

F OR YEAR-ROUND seedling cultivation, the rolling light tray is ideal. Simple to construct, it will save you hundreds of dollars compared to a commercial version. With the light tray you will discover the potential that fluorescent lights have for the indoor gardener. This tray may be just the first step in a full-scale indoor light garden that allows you to raise plants and create gardens that you thought were possible only for outdoor gardeners living in sun-kissed locales.

Tools and Materials

- Enough flexible plastic sheeting to cover the bottom and sides of the tray
- Eight ¾" × ¾" plastic or wood strips to support the flats
- Four swivelling wheels
- Sixteen #6 1" screws
- Twenty-four #6 1¼" screws
- Four commercial shelf supports or pieces of doweling
- One 4' fluorescent light
- A heavy duty stapler
- Level
- (A) One piece of ½" × 47¾" × 22" plywood
- (B) Two pieces of ½" × 48¾" × 1¼" plywood
- (C) Two pieces of ½" × 22" × 1¼" plywood
- (D) Two pieces of ½" × 20¼" × 8" plywood
- (E) Four pieces of ¾" × 20¼" × 2" solid wood
- (F) Two pieces of ¾" × 23" × 2" solid wood
- (G) Two pieces of ¾" × 51¾" × 2" solid wood

Method

1. Cut the plywood for the bottom to size (47¾" × 22"). This size will fit four standard flats.
2. Cut plywood sides (B) and ends (C).
3. Attach pieces (C) and then (D) with #6 1" screws.
4. Attach the plastic liner, tucking it into the corners and stapling it to the top edges of the sides and the ends.
5. Cut out the light support pieces (D), measuring 20¼" × 8". Drill the holes in them as shown. Space the supports approximately 6" apart, making sure they are level. It is easier to make sure they are level if you drill both pieces together.
6. Cut pieces (E), (F), and (G) to the sizes specified. Pre-drill two small holes near the end of each piece.
7. Screw the pieces (F) to (E), ensuring they are square to one another.

8. Attach the joined pieces (E) and (F) to the bottom as shown.
9. Attach pieces (G) to the tops as shown.
10. Attach piece (D) at the top and bottom.
11. Insert the shelf supports into the appropriate holes.
12. Attach the wheels.

Note: Another unit can be built on top of this one. To attach a second unit for a two-tier light tray, screw triangular braces to pieces (E) and (B), or pieces (G) and (E) to prevent it from collapsing.

Use your rolling light unit to start seedlings for spring plantings or to force blooms, or otherwise provide the right conditions for plants with exacting heat, light, and humidity requirements.

Sources &
Contributors

Art Glass Source

PO Box 4104

Clifton Park, NY 12605

USA

Toll Free Number: 800-405-6363

Ph: 518-371-0977

F: 518-371-9423

E-mail: ags-info@artglass-cource.com

Web site: www.artglass-source.com

An excellent resource for mosaic and other glass work supplies and tools. On-line and printed catalog available.

Banta Brothers Woodworking

Aaron and Scott Banta

PO Box 2641

Smithers, BC V0J 2N0

Canada

Ph: 250-847-2363

Source for garden and plant accessories including many of the projects found in this book. Specializing in fine woodworking, including Japanese-style furnishings and lamps, and a range of gardening and landscaping services.

Beadworks

Westcroft Beadworks®
149 Water St.
Norwalk, CT 06853
USA
Ph: 203-852-9108
F: 203-855-8015
Fine copper wire by the spool and other beading supplies available through catalogue.

Brainforest Design

Gail Hourigan
236 East 32nd Ave.
Vancouver, BC V5V 2Y2
Canada
Ph: 604-873-4073
Specializing in innovative crafts in fabric, including plant bags, coffee cozies, tassels, gift bags, and more.

Country Beads

2015 West 4th Ave.
Vancouver, BC V6J 1N3
Canada
Ph: 604-730-8056
Full selection of beads and beading supplies.

CP Commercial Plastics Inc.

3917 Grant St.
Burnaby, BC V5C 3N4
Canada
Ph: 604-298-1945
Website: www.complas.com
Suppliers of plastics, including Lexan. Will take individual orders.

Fascinating Folds

PO Box 10070
Glendale, AZ 85318
USA
Ph: 800-968-2418
Full range of decoupage and other paper art supplies.

Garden Web

The Internet's Gardening Community
Web site: www.gardenweb.com
Forums, event listings, tips, on a huge variety of indoor and
outdoor gardening topics.

Grand Prix Hobbies and Crafts

3038 West Broadway
Vancouver, BC
Canada
Ph: 604-733-7114
Excellent selection of paints, faux finishing supplies, and
other items.

Jim's Orchid Supplies

4157 Lebanon Rd.
Fort Pierce, FL 84982
USA
Ph: 561-489-0859
F: 810-314-4253
E-mail: orchiddj@gte.net
Web site: www.jimsupplies.com
Supplier of tree ferns, wire, rock wool, sponge rock, baskets,
ventilation and circulation supplies and more.

Kelley's Korner Orchid Supplies

PO Box 6

Kittery, ME 03904-0006

USA

Ph: 207-439-0922

F: 207-439-8202

Web site: www.ccsme.com

E-mail: kelkos@nh.ultranet.com

Orchid supplies including containers, growing medium, hangers, clips and hooks.

Wee Tree Farm

5340 NE Hwy 20

Corvallis, OR 97330-9235

USA

Toll Free Number: 800-638-1098

Ph: 541-752-1098

F: 541-752-3431

E-mail: diane@weetree.com

Web site: www.weetree.com

Japanese and Korean bonsai pottery, wire, kits, tools and more.

Wire Sculptor's Bulletin Boards

106 Highway 190 W.

Suite 143

Slidell, LA 70460

USA

E-mail: preston@wire-sculpture.com

Web site: wire-sculpture.com

An Internet and mail order resource for wire workers. Find a complete line of wire working tools, as well as advice on types of wire and wireworking techniques